# ROSICRU[

## An Introduction

*Fourteen lectures given in Munich*
*between 22 May and 6 June 1907*

Rudolf Steiner

RUDOLF STEINER PRESS

Translation revised by J. Collis

Rudolf Steiner Press
Hillside House, The Square
Forest Row, East Sussex
RH18 5ES

www.rudolfsteinerpress.com

Published by Rudolf Steiner Press 2000
Reprinted 2001

Previously published in English as *Theosophy of the Rosicrucian*
by Rudolf Steiner Press

Originally published in German under the title *Die Theosophie des Rosenkreuzers* (volume 99 in the *Rudolf Steiner Gesamtausgabe* or Collected Works) by Rudolf Steiner Verlag, Dornach. This authorized translation is published by kind permission of the Rudolf Steiner Nachlassverwaltung, Dornach

A catalogue record for this book is available from the British Library

ISBN 1 85584 063 4

Cover by Andrew Morgan
Typeset by DP Photosetting, Aylesbury, Bucks.
Printed and bound in Great Britain by Cromwell Press Limited, Trowbridge, Wilts.

# Contents

# Introduction

The term Rosicrucianism is by no means foreign to the broad spectrum of spirituality today. In this course of lectures, given comparatively early in the lecturing phase of his career, Rudolf Steiner introduces those aspects of Rosicrucianism on which spiritual science (one of Steiner's terms for the body of research that resulted from his work) has light to shed and with which it is intricately connected.

Though containing a wealth of insight into the spiritual content of Rosicrucian wisdom and practice, it seems fair to describe what is contained in this volume as only an *introduction*, if one bears in mind Steiner's contention that, if the fulness that lies behind such spiritual wisdom were to be described extensively, a 'new language' would have to be 'invented'. This was clearly not Steiner's immediate task: indeed, his vocabulary and syntax can be followed with lucidity by the kind of mind for which such ideas are entirely new, or by those who consider themselves as mere beginners on the inner path of development. At the same time, fourteen lectures make a sizeable volume when transcribed in this way, so that when one has finished reading the last page, there can be little doubt qualitatively that the *whole* must be reflected fully—if not contained—in this 'introductory' *part*.

What might the most intrinsic components of that 'whole' be? Since Steiner is not writing a systematic survey of Rosicrucian wisdom, ideally each person would need to crystallize this from the lecture course for themselves. An Introduction such as this may serve, however, to enable the reader, the enquirer or the student to be able to embark on this crystallization process more effectively—rather in the sense that a good guide will enable the visitor to gain a fuller experience, say, of Botticelli's *Primavera* than would otherwise be gained from the necessarily brief visit to the Uffizi that most hectic tourist schedules in Florence permit.

Which leads us directly into one of the components of the spiritual stream of Rosicrucianism with which Steiner is concerned. It is a body of knowledge (or even mode of living) ideally suited to the 'busy' person whose life nevertheless is self-motivated by a wish or resolve to find practical ways of alleviating world problems—solving them might be too presumptuous a claim, though it is obviously what ultimately needs to come about.

Though Steiner deals elsewhere with the historical background that is directly concerned with the being of Christian Rosencreutz, the individuality after whom Rosicrucianism is named, here it is clearly not his immediate concern. However, in the last lecture, he does point out that the spiritual source from which all later esoteric training derives can be traced back to the Athenian teacher, and pupil of St. Paul: Dionysius the Areopagite. Corroboratively, a hint of this occurs in I Cor. ii 6–7, in which Paul speaks of 'Theosophia', the wisdom of God, the same term having been used in the original German title (and in the title of the earlier translation of the lectures into English): *Die Theosophie des Rosenkreuzers*, a term which was superseded for Steiner by 'anthroposophy' when he distanced himself from certain ideas being promulgated by leading theosophists in the years shortly after this lecture course took place. 'Howbeit we speak wisdom among them that are perfect: yet not the wisdom of this world, nor of the princes of this world, that came to nought: But we speak the *wisdom of God* in a mystery, even the hidden wisdom, which God ordained before this world unto our glory'. (The King James version, my emphasis).

This aspect of Rosicrucianism, however, its esoteric training ('hidden wisdom' as the translation puts it), is not one that Steiner is content merely to make passing reference to: in so far as it is possible to go into such detail he describes the seven stages on this inner path. Furthermore, he makes it abundantly clear that the training is distinct from what he calls the Christian path, a fact which could, in the first place, be of central importance for many people today—the distinction notwithstanding all that he had to divulge about the Christ Being on numerous occasions elsewhere or, perhaps even more paradoxical, his allusion to the Pauline roots of esoteric training.

This is not the place to rehearse the seven stages, let alone expand on them. Suffice it to say, however, that, as the first stage is designated *study*, one could consider the whole 'book' as an example of how to set about placing one's first footstep upon this path. Not that Steiner fences in a number of fields of study and sets about devoting one lecture to each of them. Despite the helpful titles to each lecture and the build up of the body of knowledge that results, Steiner's style of lecturing—which makes it so refreshing for the modern thinker—is one in which he ranges freely around his core theme. This may well be the result of having to give the listener access to concepts for which the 'new language' has not been invented. Do we not find poets constantly attempting something similar through the use of metaphor and imagery?—though frequently they may have to stop short at, as well as coin, language that does little more than offer a peep-hole of a perspective towards the ineffability that they divine, however strong their divining might be?

Perhaps this mode of 'study' could best be exemplified by looking at the problems of the day to which Steiner alludes—though he does so seemingly with little more than passing reference—by seeing, in view of his contention that modern

Rosicrucianism is a way of bringing spiritual wisdom into the service of practical life, in what ways he addresses the problems. Not that Steiner has quick-fix solutions to offer. Nor that he structures the lecture course into compartments that neatly consider each problem in turn. His aim rather is to open up the broad horizon of Rosicrucian wisdom, culminating, as already mentioned, in the final lecture in which he speaks about the inner path of one who would seek further for solutions to the problematic situations that life presents, where individuals may earnestly feel drawn towards making a contribution out of themselves.

The problems which Steiner cites are: education, the social question, medicine, food and feminism. For some, these may come as a surprise: it was still only 1907! Could the shortlist of priorities, given slightly updated wording, be so very different at the turn of the millennium, 93 years and two world wars later? There surely cannot be many editions of the *New York Times* that are silent even on one of these counts. Yet it does not at all come across that Steiner was assuming airs of prophecy. There is no suggestion that unless the Rosicrucian approach be considered and taken practically into account the problems that at present gnaw into the heart of society will not retreat. Nonetheless, not only have they not retreated, but one can experience them advancing on several fronts, sometimes, nay frequently, drastically.

Hence is to be found, *passim* throughout all fourteen lectures, the Rosicrucian approach to each of these pressing questions with which humanity wrestles. The approach presents, as might be expected, a common method for each situation, at least at the outset, which could be summarized as follows: to look comprehensively at the phenomena; to identify which of these are particularly significant; to remain 'passive' as far as feelings are concerned (feelings will play their part later); to allow the phenomena to impress themselves upon one's inner being—to let them 'speak'; and from this to research the relative field of wisdom from which a solution will need to be drawn; and, when this field is sufficiently and assuredly within sight, and one's feelings of conviction and compassion also having achieved the necessary degree of objectivity, then to determine the best way to act.

It would be naive to think of the healing of society's ills as anything other than a very long haul and requiring a commensurately long-term commitment. Nor is this the place to do more than mention the value—indeed, often the *necessity*— of shorter-term 'plasters' that are often called for when the immediacy of a situation cannot humanly wait for the long-term solution. Here again, the Rosicrucian path offers consolation: the first step towards acquiring the necessary wisdom in action being *study*, one can, if one is so minded, begin with deliberation at once, and at each stage of progress a proportionately valuable harvest may be reaped.

This brings us back again to the lectures as a whole, themselves more than a glimpse into the Rosicrucian treasure-chest of spiritual knowledge that Steiner begins to open up—the nature of the child's incarnating as a vital part of the background to the educational question; the course of human evolution as part of the background to the social question and the steps needed to move towards global 'brotherliness', understanding and tolerance; the complex constitution of the two sexes as part of the background to the feminist question (with all its repercussions that transpired as the century advanced); and so on.

So much for the main substance that the lectures provide for all, though no doubt individual readers will come across 'cherries in the cake' that are a particular delight or that lead to particularly awakening insights: e.g. that the heart muscles are structured in the same way as those used for *voluntary* acts; that the spread of spiritual knowledge can of itself provide the foundation for love in the future; that the fidgetiness, so prevalent in the modern classroom, has roots in the past (as well as all that is laid at the threshold of many modern life-styles); that the mythologies of past cultures derive from a form of consciousness that is *essentially* different from the one we exercise in our mundane life today, but one that would have future significance if we could regain it, not by reverting to an earlier state, but by *extending* what we have so far achieved on this long—and humanly precarious—'road to freedom'. And there is, of course, much more.

The knowledge of 'higher worlds' can often seem to have little relevance when one is embroiled in the crammed cra-ziness of the rush-hour, in coping with the rising tide of leg-islation, in the trauma of a divorce case, in one's adolescent's drug problems, in the GM tug-of-war going on behind offi-cially required labelling, small-printed somewhere amongst all the glittering packaging of the supermarket, in the flick-ering TV images of forlorn refugees in so many parts of the globe, in the soul-searing reports one reads of the acts of porn-polluted paedophiles, etc. A considerable volume of 'virtual' space could be increasingly jammed with these and other *realities* (*sic*) that continuously beset us.

But it is contrary to the Rosicrucian way to go into any sort of ascetic retreat in the face of personal trials or world dis-asters, on however large or small a scale they may be. For those concerned with seeking solutions to current problems—or simply with achieving compassionate insight, if that seems as much as can be done at present—this course of Rudolf Steiner's lectures opens up the way to new resources and potential.

Brien Masters
Winter Solstice 1999

Lecture 1

# The New Form of Wisdom

The title of this course of lectures has been announced as 'Theosophy according to the Rosicrucian Method'. By this is meant the wisdom that is primeval, yet ever new, expressed in a form suitable for the present age. The mode of thought we are about to study has existed since the fourteenth century AD. In these lectures, however, it is not my intention to speak of the history of Rosicrucianism.

As you know, a certain kind of geometry which includes, for instance, the Theorem of Pythagoras, is taught in elementary schools today. The rudiments of geometry are learnt quite independently of how geometry itself actually came into being, for what does the pupil who is learning the rudiments of geometry today know about Euclid? Nevertheless it is Euclid's geometry that is being taught. Not until later, when the substance has been mastered, do students discover, perhaps from a history of the sciences, something about the form in which the teaching that is accessible even in elementary schools today originally found its way into the evolution of humanity. As little as the pupil who learns elementary geometry today is concerned with the form in which it was originally given to humanity by Euclid, as little need we concern ourselves with the question of how Rosicrucianism developed in the course of history. Just as the pupil learns geometry from its actual tenets, so shall we learn to know the nature of this Rosicrucian wisdom from its intrinsic principles.

Those who are acquainted merely with the outer history of Rosicrucianism, as recorded in literature, know very little about the real content of Rosicrucian theosophy or wisdom.

Rosicrucian wisdom has existed since the fourteenth century as something that is true, quite apart from its history, just as geometrical truths exist independently of history. Only a fleeting reference, therefore, will here be made to certain matters connected with the history of Rosicrucianism.

In 1459 a lofty spiritual individuality, incarnate in the human personality who bears in the world the name of Christian Rosenkreuz, appeared as the teacher of a small circle of initiated pupils. In 1459, within a strictly secluded spiritual brotherhood, the *Fraternitas Rosae Crucis*, Christian Rosenkreuz was raised to the rank of *Eques lapidis aurei*, Knight of the Golden Stone. What this means will become clearer to us in the course of these lectures. The exalted individual who lived on the physical plane in the personality of Christian Rosenkreuz worked as leader and teacher of the Rosicrucian stream 'again and again in the same body', as esotericism puts it. The meaning of the expression 'again and again in the same body' will also be explained when we come to speak of the destiny of the human being after death.

Until far into the eighteenth century, the wisdom of which we are speaking was preserved within a secret brotherhood, bound by strict rules which separated its members from the exoteric world.

In the eighteenth century it was the mission of this brotherhood to allow certain esoteric truths to flow, by spiritual ways, into the culture of Central Europe. That is why we see flashing up in an exoteric culture many things that are clothed, it is true, in an exoteric form, but which are, in reality, nothing else than outer expressions of esoteric wisdom.

In the course of the centuries a good many people have endeavoured, in one way or another, to discover the Rosicrucian wisdom, but they did not succeed. Leibniz, for example, tried in vain to get at the source of this wisdom.[1] Yet Rosicrucian wisdom did light up like a flash of lightning in an exoteric work which appeared when Lessing was approaching the close of his life.[2] I refer to Lessing's *Education of the Human Race*. Reading between the lines—if we are esotericists—we can recognize by its singular ending that it is an external expression of Rosicrucian wisdom.

This wisdom lit up in outstanding grandeur in the man in whom European culture, and indeed international culture, was reflected at the turn of the eighteenth century—in Goethe.[3] While he was still comparatively young, Goethe had come into contact with a source of Rosicrucianism and he then experienced, in some degree, a very remarkable and lofty initiation. To speak of initiation in connection with Goethe may easily be misleading, so it is appropriate to mention something extraordinary that happened to him during the period after he had left Leipzig University and before he went to Strasbourg. He underwent an experience that penetrated very deeply into his soul and expressed itself outwardly in the fact that during the last period of his stay in Leipzig he came very near to death. As he lay desperately ill he had a momentous experience, passing through a kind of initiation. He was not actually conscious of it at first but it worked in his soul as a kind of poetic inspiration, and the process by which it flowed into his various creations was most remarkable. It flashes up in his poem entitled 'The Mysteries', which his closest friends considered to be one of his most profound creations.[4] This fragment is indeed so profound that Goethe was never able to recapture the power to formulate its conclusion. The culture of the day was incapable of giving external form to the depths of life pulsating in this poem. It must be regarded as coming from one of the deepest founts of Goethe's soul, and is a book with seven seals for all his commentators. As time went on the initiation worked its way increasingly into his awareness and finally, as he grew more conscious of it, he was able to produce that remarkable prose-poem known as 'The Fairy Tale of the Green Snake and the Beautiful Lily'—one of the most profound writings in all literature.[5] Those who are able to interpret it rightly, know a great deal of Rosicrucian wisdom.

At the time when Rosicrucian wisdom was intended to flow gradually into the general life of culture, it happened, in a manner of which I need not speak further now, that a kind of betrayal took place. Certain Rosicrucian conceptions found their way into the world at large. This betrayal on the one hand, and on the other the fact that it was necessary for nineteenth-century Western culture to remain for a time on the physical plane, uninfluenced by esotericism—these two facts made it imperative that the sources of Rosicrucian wisdom, and above all its great founder, who since its inception had been constantly on the physical plane, should apparently withdraw. Thus during the first half and also during a large part of the second half of the nineteenth century, little of Rosicrucian wisdom could be discovered. Only now, in our own time, has it become possible to make this Rosicrucian wisdom accessible again and allow it to flow into general culture. If we think about this culture we shall discover the reasons why this had to be.

I will now speak of two characteristics of Rosicrucian wisdom which are important in connection with its mission in the world. One has to do with people's whole attitude towards this Rosicrucian wisdom—which is not the same thing as the esoteric form of Christian-Gnostic wisdom. We must touch briefly upon two facts pertaining to the spiritual life if we are to be clear about the fundamental character of Rosicrucian wisdom. The first of these is the relationship of the pupil to the teacher; and here again there are two aspects to consider. We shall speak, first, of what is termed 'clairvoyance', and secondly, of what is called 'belief in authority'. 'Clairvoyance'—the term is really inadequate—comprises not only spiritual seeing but also spiritual hearing. These two faculties are the source of all knowledge of the world's hidden wisdom, and true knowledge of the spiritual worlds can come from no other source.

In Rosicrucianism there is an essential difference between discovering spiritual truths and understanding them. Only those who have developed spiritual faculties in a fairly high degree can themselves discover a spiritual truth in the higher worlds. Clairvoyance is the necessary prerequisite for discovering a spiritual truth, but only for discovering it. For a long time to come, nothing will be taught exoterically by any genuine Rosicrucianism that cannot be grasped by the ordinary, logical intellect. That is the essential point. The objection that clairvoyance is necessary for understanding the Rosicrucian form of wisdom is not valid. Understanding does not depend upon the faculty of seership. Those who are incapable of grasping Rosicrucian wisdom with their thinking have simply not developed their logical reasoning powers to a sufficient extent—that is all. Anyone who has absorbed all that modern culture is able to give, who is not too lazy to learn and has patience and perseverance, can understand what a Rosicrucian teacher has to impart. Those who have doubts about Rosicrucian wisdom and who say that they cannot grasp it, must not blame this on their inability to rise to higher planes. The fault lies in their unwillingness either to exert their reasoning powers sufficiently or to put experiences gained from general culture to adequate use.

Just think of the tremendous popularization of wisdom that has taken place since the appearance of Christianity down to the present day, and then try to picture Christian Rosicrucianism as it was in the fourteenth century. Think of the relation of a human being, then living in the world, with his teachers. It was only possible to work by means of the spoken word in those days. On the whole we fail to appreciate what tremendous development has taken place since that time. Think only of what has resulted from the invention of printing. Think of the thousands and thousands of channels through which, thanks to that invention, the highest achievements of culture have been able to flow into civilization. From books down to the most trivial newspaper article, you can perceive the innumerable channels through which countless ideas flow into life. These channels have only been open for humanity since that time, and they have had the effect of making the western intellect assume quite different forms. The western mind has worked quite differently since then, and the new form of wisdom had necessarily to reckon with this fact.

A form had to be created which would be able to stand its ground in face of all that flows into life along these thousands of channels. Rosicrucian wisdom can hold its own against any objection, whether popular or highly scientific. Rosicrucian wisdom contains within itself the sources which enable it to counter every objection made by science. A true understanding of modern science, not the dilettante understanding to be found even among university professors, but understanding that is free from abstract theorizing and materialistic conjectures and is founded firmly upon facts and does not go beyond them, can find from science itself the proofs of the spiritual truths of Rosicrucianism.

A second point concerning the relationship between teacher and pupil in Rosicrucianism is that the relationship of the pupil to the 'guru' (as the teacher is called in the East) is fundamentally different from that prevailing in other methods of initiation. In Rosicrucianism this relationship cannot in any way be said to be based upon belief in a superior authority. Let me make this clear to you by an example drawn from everyday life. The Rosicrucian teacher wants a relationship with his pupil which is like that of a mathematics teacher with his students. Can it be said that students of mathematics look up to their teacher simply out of a belief in authority? No! And can it be said that students of mathematics do not need the teacher? Some people may argue that they do not, because they may have discovered how to teach themselves from good books. However, that situation differs from the one in which a student and teacher sit face to face. In principle, of course, self-instruction is possible. Equally, every human being, provided he reaches a certain stage of clairvoyance, can discover spiritual truths for himself, but this would be a much more lengthy path. It would be senseless to say: My own inner being must be the sole source of all spiritual truths. If the teacher knows mathematical truths and imparts them to his pupils, the pupils no longer need to have a 'belief in authority' for they grasp these truths through the correctness inherent in them, and all they need do is understand them. So is it with all esoteric development in the Rosicrucian sense. The teacher is the friend, the counsellor, one who has already lived through esoteric experiences and now helps the pupils to do so themselves. Once someone has had these experiences there is as little need for him to accept things on authority as there is in mathematics for him to accept on authority the statement that the three angles of a triangle add up to 180 degrees. In Rosicrucianism there is no 'authority' in the ordinary sense. It is simply a question of what is required for shortening the path to the highest truths.

That is the one side of the question; the other is the relation of spiritual wisdom to culture in general.

These lectures will show you that it is possible for truth to flow directly into practical life. We are not setting up a system that is applicable in theory only; we are speaking of teachings which can be put to use in practical life by anyone who desires to know the deeper foundations of present-day worldly knowledge, and which allow spiritual truths to flow into everyday life. Rosicrucian wisdom must not stream only into the head, nor only into the heart, but also into the hand, into our manual skills, into our daily actions. It does not take effect as sentimental sympathy; it is the acquisition, by strenuous effort, of faculties enabling us to work for the well-being of humanity. Suppose some society were to proclaim human brotherhood as its aim and were to do no more than preach brotherhood. That would not be Rosicrucianism, for the Rosicrucian says: Imagine someone lying in the road with a broken leg. If fourteen people stand around him in pity but not one of them is able to help, the whole fourteen together are of less importance than a fifteenth who comes, perhaps without any sentimentality at all, but is able to, and actually does, deal with the broken leg.

The attitude of the Rosicrucian is that what counts is knowledge able to take hold of and intervene effectively in life. Rosicrucian wisdom considers that repeated talk about pity and sympathy has an element of danger in it, for continual harping on sympathy denotes a kind of astral sensuality. Sensuality on the physical plane is of the same nature as, on the astral plane, the constant wish to feel but never to know. Knowledge that is capable of taking effect in practical life— not, of course in the materialistic sense, but because it is brought down from spiritual worlds—this is what enables us to work effectively. Harmony flows of itself from the knowledge that the world must progress; and it flows all the more surely because it arises quite naturally out of knowledge. You could say of someone who knows how do deal with a broken leg but does not do so that he neglects the sufferer because he dislikes people. Such a thing would be possible in the case of knowledge pertaining only to the physical plane. But it would not be possible for spiritual knowledge. There is no spiritual knowledge that would refrain from entering into practical life.

This, then, is the second aspect of Rosicrucian wisdom,

namely, that although it can be discovered only through the powers of clairvoyance, it can be understood by normal human reason. It may seem strange to say that in order to have experiences in the spiritual world you must become clairvoyant, but that you need not be clairvoyant in order to understand what the clairvoyant sees. A seer who returns from the spiritual worlds and tells of what is going on there— bringing people knowledge that is necessary for humanity at the present time—can be understood if those who listen are willing to understand, for human beings are constituted in a way that makes it possible for them to understand.

We shall begin by studying the sevenfold nature of the human being according to Rosicrucian teaching. We shall consider the whole of human nature as we see it before us; we shall learn to understand the nature of the physical body about which so many think they know everything while in fact they know nothing. As little as we can see the oxygen in water but must separate it from the hydrogen in order to recognize it, as little do we see the real physical human being when we look at someone standing before us. The human being is a combination of physical body, ether body, astral body and the other higher members, just as water is a combination of oxygen and hydrogen. The being before us is the sum total of all these members. If we are to see the physical body alone, the astral body must have separated from it: this is the condition in dreamless sleep. Sleep is a kind of higher chemical separation of the astral body, together with the higher members of our nature, from the etheric and physical bodies. But even then it cannot be said that we have the real physical body before us. The physical body is alone only at death, when the ether body too has left it.

This has a direct and concrete bearing. I will make it clear to you by means of an example. Think of some particular part of the astral body. In the remote past, the pictures which the human being perceived in dim, shadowy clairvoyance worked very differently than do mental images today. These pictures were impressed, first of all, into the astral body. Let us suppose that at one time pictures of the three dimensions of space—length, breadth, depth—were impressed into the astral body. This picture of three-dimensional space, which was once impressed into the astral body through the old, dim clairvoyance, was carried over into the ether body. Just as a seal is pressed into liquid sealing wax, so did the astral picture impress itself into the ether body, which in turn moulded the forms of the physical body. Thus the picture of three-dimensional space built an organ in a particular area of the physical body. Originally there was a picture in the astral body of the three perpendicular directions of space; this picture impressed itself, like a seal into wax, into the ether body and a certain part of the ether body moulded an organ in the interior of the human ear, namely the three semi-circular canals. You all have them within you; if they are in any way impaired you cannot orientate yourself within the three directions of space: you get giddy and cannot stand upright. Thus are the pictures of the astral body connected with the forces of the ether body and the organs of the physical body.

The whole way that the human physical body is shaped is nothing else than a product of the pictures of the astral body and the forces of the ether body. Hence those who have no knowledge of the astral and ether bodies cannot understand the physical body. The astral body is the predecessor of the ether body and the ether body is the predecessor of the physical body. This is how complicated these things are.

The three semi-circular canals are a physical organ, just as is the nose. All noses differ from one another although there may be a resemblance between the noses of parents and children. If you were able to study the three semi-circular canals inside the human ear, you would find differences and resemblances just as in the case of noses, for these canals may resemble those of one's mother or father. What is not inherited is the innermost spirit, the eternal core which passes through successive incarnations. Individual talents and capacities are not determined by the brain. Logic is what it is: it is the same in mathematics, in philosophy, or in practical life. Differences in capacity only appear when logic is applied in areas involving particular physical organs; where knowledge depends, for instance, upon the functioning of the semicircular canals in the ear. Mathematical talent will be particularly marked when these organs are highly developed. An example of this is the Bernoulli family which produced a succession of fine mathematicians.[6] An individual may possess great incipient talent for music or some other art, but if he is not born into a human body that has inherited the requisite organic structures, he cannot bring these talents to expression.

So you see, the physical world cannot be understood without knowledge of how it is constituted. The Rosicrucian does not consider it his task to withdraw in any way from the physical world. Certainly not! For what he has to do is to spiritualize the physical world. He must rise to the highest regions of spiritual life and with the knowledge there obtained labour actively in the physical world, especially amongst human beings.

This is the Rosicrucian attitude—the direct outcome of Rosicrucian wisdom. We are about to study a system of wisdom which will enable us to understand even the smallest things; and we shall not forget that the smallest thing in the world can be of importance to the greatest, that the smallest thing, in its rightful place, can lead to the highest of goals!

# Lecture 2

# The Ninefold Constitution of the Human Being

In the previous lecture we spoke of the kind of relationship Rosicrucianism adopts towards the human being and culture in general. Although actual knowledge concerning the higher worlds can be discovered only by the seer, by more highly developed spiritual faculties, nevertheless the Rosicrucian method is such that the wisdom it imparts can be understood by the logical intellect. The knowledge itself is discovered by a seer with higher faculties, but normal human reason is capable of comprehending it. Let it not be imagined, however, that what it is possible to say in a single lecture can hold its own against all criticism; this could only be so if the statements were put to the test by all the means accessible to the human mind. In the last lecture we also spoke about another characteristic of Rosicrucianism, namely that this method aims at carrying spiritual science into practical life. That is why things are expressed here in such a way that they can be made an integral part of life. Here, too, you must have patience, for initially it will seem as though many things are inapplicable in practical life. But when you are able to survey the whole, you will realize that what I have said is true. The Rosicrucian method of investigation is able to impart wisdom that can take effect in life.

First of all we will consider the several members of which the human being consists. Only by advancing step by step and omitting nothing shall we be able to get a view of the organic whole. We shall also study the destiny of the human soul after death and the human being in waking consciousness, in sleep and in death. We shall have to consider what is accomplished by human beings between death and a new birth. It is a widespread view that they are inactive after death, but the contrary is the case. They have to be intensely active, to create, to perform work that is important for the cosmos. We shall also have to speak of reincarnation and karma, of destiny in human evolution, of how humanity developed in times gone by and of evolution in the future.

Today it will be my task to give a brief description of the constitution and nature of the human being. We must realize that the nature and being of man appear far more complex to spiritual perception than to ordinary sense-perception, which is interwoven with intellect and can only observe a very small portion of human nature as a whole. From the esoteric point of view, the physical body as we see it before us is permeated by the ether and astral bodies. These three bodies are united, and only when the other two are removed do we have the real physical body before us. The physical body is that member which the human being has in common with the whole of physical nature consisting of minerals, plants and animals.

The only correct view of the physical body is to say that it corresponds with the extent of the human being's kinship with the surrounding mineral kingdom. But you must realize that this member of the human being is the one that can least of all be conceived of as separate from the cosmos. The forces working in the physical body pour in from the cosmos. Think of a rainbow. If a rainbow is to appear, there must be a particular combination of sunlight, rainclouds and so on. The rainbow cannot be absent if this combination between sunlight and rainclouds exists. The rainbow is therefore a consequence, a phenomenon brought into being from without. The physical body too is, in a way, a pure phenomenon. You must look in the whole surrounding universe for the forces which hold the physical body together. Where can we find, in their true form, these forces that cause the physical body to have the appearance it has? The answer leads us into higher worlds, for in the physical world we see the physical body as a phenomenon only. The forces that give rise to this phenomenon lie in a very lofty spiritual world. We must therefore give some study to worlds that exist as truly as the physical world exists.

When spiritual researchers speak of higher worlds they mean worlds that are around us all the time, only the senses for perceiving them must be opened just as the eyes must be opened for the perception of colours. When certain senses of the soul, senses that lie a degree higher than the physical senses, are opened, the world around us is pervaded by a new revelation known as the astral world. Rosicrucian theosophy or wisdom calls this world the Imaginative World—but 'Imaginative' here denotes something much more real than that word normally implies. There is a constant flowing and ebbing of pictures; colours that are otherwise chained to objects are involved in myriad transformations within the astral world. In the movement that has linked itself with Rosicrucianism this world is also called the 'elemental world'. These three expressions therefore—Imaginative world, astral world, elemental world—are interchangeable.

A still loftier world, revealed to yet higher senses, is that of the 'harmonies of the spheres'. This higher world penetrates into the world of pictures and colours. It is called 'Devachan', 'Rupa Devachan', or also the 'mental world'; in Rosicrucian terminology it is known as the world of the 'harmonies of the spheres' or the 'world of Inspiration', because musical sound is the medium of Inspiration when the corresponding senses have been opened. In the movement that has linked itself with Rosicrucianism, this world has been called the 'heaven-world'. Lower or Rupa-Devachanic world, Devachan, the world of Inspiration, the heaven-world—these again are one and the same.

An even higher world, revealed by yet higher senses, is known in Rosicrucianism as the world of true Intuition, but 'Intuition' here has a much higher reality than is contained in the word as used in everyday life. True Intuition is a 'merging into' other beings, so that they are known from within themselves. In the movement that has linked itself with Rosicrucianism, this world of Intuition has been called the 'world of reason'; it is so far above the ordinary world that it casts only a shadow-image into the world of human beings. Intellectual concepts are faint and feeble shadow-images of the realities in this higher world.

So in addition to the physical world there are three other worlds. Behind the forces which hold the physical world together there are forces that are to be found in the highest world, the world of Intuition. In comparison with the beings and forces in this highest world, everything that the physicist discovers in the physical world is like so many faint shadow-images. For every concept you have, say, of a crystal or of the human eye, you would find living entities in this highest world. A concept in the physical world is the shadow-image of entities in this highest world. Thus the physical world is built up of forces which manifest in their true form in Arupa-Devachan—to use the theosophical mode of expression.

We can form a still clearer conception if we think about the mineral kingdom from this point of view. The human being has a consciousness of the ego, 'I'-consciousness. We say that a mineral is without consciousness, but this is true only on the physical plane. In the higher worlds the mineral is not without consciousness. You will not, however, find the ego of the mineral world in the elemental world; the ego-consciousness of the mineral lies in the highest of the worlds of which we have spoken. Just as your finger has no consciousness of its own, for its consciousness lies in your 'I' or ego, so the mineral is connected with its ego by currents that lead into the very highest realm of world-existence. A finger-nail is part of the human organism as a whole; its consciousness is in the 'I' or ego. A finger-nail is related to the organism as the mineral is related to the highest spiritual world. There is one 'I' or ego belonging to the whole living organism, and the nails, like the mineral, are an outermost manifestation of what has hardened within this life.

The human physical body has this in common with the minerals: that the physical body, in so far as it is purely physical, has a consciousness belonging to it in the spiritual world above. Inasmuch as the human being is endowed with purely physical consciousness (although he does not know it), inasmuch as he has a physical body with its consciousness in a higher world, his constitution is such that the physical body is worked upon from above. What fashions your physical body is not under your control. Just as it is the 'I' or ego that moves your hand, so is your physical body worked upon from a higher world, and the ego-consciousness belonging to the physical body gives rise to the physical processes of the body. The initiate who attains to Intuition is the only one who has such power over his physical body that no current passes through his nerves without his knowledge; not until an individual reaches this stage can he be a companion of those spiritual beings up there who govern and direct his physical body.

The human being has his second member, the ether body or life body, in common with the plants and animals. It is visible to the seer and has approximately the same form as the physical body. It is a body of forces. If you could think away the physical body, the ether body would be left as a body of forces, a body permeated with lines of force that have built up the physical body. The human heart could never have assumed the form it bears if there were not in the ether body an etheric heart; this etheric heart contains certain forces and currents and these are the builders, the architects, the moulders of the physical heart. Suppose you had a vessel containing water and you were to cool the water until hardenings, ice-formations appeared in it. The ice is water, only the water has hardened and the shapes of the ice-blocks were already within the water as lines of force. Thus is the physical heart formed out of the etheric heart; it is simply a hardened etheric heart and the streams of force in the etheric heart have given the physical heart its shape.

If you could think away the physical body, you would see that the ether body, especially in the upper parts, is fairly similar to the physical body. This similarity, however, continues only as far as the middle of the body, for there is also a great difference compared with the physical body. You will understand what this is when I tell you that the ether body in a man is female and in a woman male. Without this knowledge much will remain incomprehensible in everyday life. Another characteristic is that the ether body appears like a form of light extending slightly beyond the shape of the physical body. The human being has the ether body in common with the plants.

The situation of the ether body resembles that of the physical body; the forces that hold the ether body together are found in the world of Inspiration, the world of Rupa-Devachan, the heaven-world. All the forces that hold the ether body together lie one stage lower than those that hold the physical body together. So you must also expect to find the ego-consciousness of the plants in this world of Inspiration, of Lower Devachan, of the harmonies of the spheres. In this same world, too, lies the ego-consciousness that pervades the human ether body and lives within you without your being aware of it.

We now come to the third member, the astral body—the 'soul body' in Rosicrucian terminology. We have our astral body in common with the animals only. The astral body is the bearer of feeling, of happiness and suffering, joy and pain, emotions and passions; wishes and desires, too, are anchored in the astral body. The astral body must be characterized by saying that there is within it something that is also present in the animal world. The animal world, too, has a consciousness. The astral being of man and of the animal is held together by forces which have their seat in the world of Imagination—or the 'elemental world' in Rosicrucian parlance. The forces that hold the astral body together and give it the form it has can be perceived in their true shape in the astral world. The ego-consciousness of the animal is also within this astral world. While in the case of a human being we speak of an individual soul, in the case of an animal we speak of a group-soul which is to be found on the astral plane. We must not think here of the single animal living on the physical plane; a whole animal species—all lions, all tigers—has an ego in common, which can be found as a group-soul on the astral plane. So the animal is really only comprehensible when it can be followed upwards to the astral plane. 'Strands', as it were, go forth from the lions, for example, and in the astral world unite into the group-soul that is common to the individual lions living on the earth.

Just as the human being has an individual ego, so in every astral body there lives something of a group-ego; this animal-ego lives in the human astral body and the human being does not become independent of this animal-ego until he develops astral sight and becomes a companion of astral beings, when the group-souls of the animals confront him on the astral plane as individual animals confront him here. In the astral world there are beings who can only come down to the physical plane in fragments, as it were, divided up into individual animals. When the life of these animals comes to an end they unite in the astral world with the rest of this astral being. A whole species of animals is a single being on the astral plane, a being with whom converse can be held as with an individual here on earth. Although there is no exact similarity, the group-souls are not incorrectly characterized in the second seal of the Apocalypse where they are divided into four classes:[7] Lion, Eagle, Bull, Man (i.e. the human being who has not yet descended to the physical plane). These four apocalyptic animals are the four classes of group-soul which are closest to the human being in his individual soul on the astral plane.

Let us now turn to what the human being does not have in common with the world around him, the being expressed in the 'I' or ego. By virtue of this fourth member, the human being is the crown of physical creation; this fourth member is what has consciousness here on the physical plane. Just as mineral consciousness is in the world of Arupa-Devachan, plant consciousness in Rupa-Devachan, and animal consciousness on the astral plane, so is human ego-consciousness in the physical world. In his 'I' or ego the human being has something into which no other being or centre of consciousness intrudes.

Thus we have the fourfold human being: physical man, etheric man, astral man, and ego or 'I'.

This does not, however, comprise the whole of human nature. Human beings had these four members in their very first incarnation on the earth, and as they pass through successive incarnations, further development takes place. They work, from their ego, upon the three other members. In the remote past, during their first incarnation on earth, human beings were entirely under the sway of every emotion and desire; although they had an ego, they behaved as animals behave. The difference between a wild individual and a highly-evolved idealist lies in the fact that the former has not yet worked from his ego upon his astral body. The next step in evolution is for human beings to work on their astral body. The result of such work is that certain fundamental properties of the astral body are brought under the individual's own control. The average European allows himself to follow certain impulses and forbids himself to yield to others. The part of his astral body that an individual has managed to bring under the control of the ego is what we call the spirit-self or manas. Manas is a product of the transformation of the astral body by the ego. In its substantiality, spirit-self is identical with the astral body; there is merely a different ordering of what was originally in the astral body but has been transformed into spirit-self.

An individual whose development progresses acquires the faculty not only of working upon his astral body but also of working from the ego upon his ether body. Let us be clear about the difference between working upon the astral body and working upon the ether body. Think of what we knew at the age, say, of eight, and of what we have learnt since then. Obviously we have learnt a great deal. Every individual has assimilated a vast number of concepts and ideas which cause him no longer to follow his emotions and passions blindly. But someone who remembers having a violent temper as a child and then thinks of how far this violent temper has been conquered, will find that it is still apt to break out. Again, it is rare for those who once had a bad memory to succeed in fundamentally improving it, or to succeed in changing character traits such as, for example, altering the strength or weakness of their conscience. I have often compared the changes people can bring about in their temperament and the like with the slow progress of the hour-hand of a clock. The essential characteristic of the pupil's initiation is this: learning is regarded as a mere preparation; much more is done for initiation when the temperament itself is transformed. If a feeble memory has been changed into a strong one, if violence has been changed into gentleness, a melancholic temperament into serenity, more has been accomplished than the acquisition of great learning. Herein lies a source of inner, esoteric powers, for this indicates that the ego is working upon the ether body, not only upon the astral body.

In so far as they express themselves, these qualities are to be found in the astral body, but if they are to be transformed, this must happen in the ether body. Whatever the ego has trans-formed in the ether body is present in the human being as life-spirit, in contrast to life-body. In theosophical literature, life-spirit is called 'buddhi'. The substantiality of buddhi is nothing else than that part of the ether body that has been transformed by the ego.

When the ego becomes so strong that it is able not only to transform the ether body, but also the physical body—the densest of the principles in the human being, the forces of which extend into the very highest world—we say that an individual is developing what is at present the very highest member of his being: spirit-man, or atma. The forces for the transformation of the physical body lie in the highest world of all. The transformation of the physical body begins with the transformation of the breathing process, for atma is breath. This transformation causes changes in the constitution of the blood which works upon the physical body; the human being is here working upwards into the very highest worlds.

Transformation can proceed in two ways, and to be precise we must speak of an unconscious and a conscious transfor-mation. In reality, every European, working from the ego, has unconsciously transformed the lower members of his being. In the present phase of evolution he works consciously only in respect of developing spirit-self (manas) and he must be an initiate if he wants to learn to transform his ether body con-sciously.

Thus we and even the most primitive human beings in the very earliest stage of evolution have the three original members and within these the ego. Then began the process of transformation. For long ages it proceeded unconsciously; but now humanity as a whole is beginning consciously to transform the astral body. Initiates meanwhile are consciously transforming the ether body and in the future all human beings will consciously transform the ether body and the physical body.

The three primeval members of our being are: physical body, ether body, astral body—and then the 'I', the ego. First the ego brings about transformation. First it transforms these three members, a process that for present-day humanity lies in the past. Unconsciously it brought about as germinal realities the sentient soul, intellectual soul and consciousness soul.[8]

Rosicrucian theosophy or wisdom makes the following distinction: sentient soul, intellectual soul, consciousness soul. The conscious process of transformation lights up for the first time in the consciousness soul. At this point the ego begins to work consciously at the transformation. First of all spirit-self is developed in the astral body. In the ether body the life-spirit is developed, as a counterpart to the life-body, and then in the physical body the actual spirit-man, atma, is developed. Thus there are in all nine members of our nature.

Outwardly regarded, two of these members—sentient soul and soul-body—are as though one inside the other, like a sword in its sheath; the sentient soul is within the soul-body, so that they appear as one. It is similar with spirit-self and consciousness soul.

These nine members are thus reduced to seven:

1. physical body
2. ether or life body
3. astral body within which is the sentient soul
4. ego.

And the higher members:

5. spirit-self (manas) together with the consciousness soul

6. life-spirit (buddhi), and as the highest
7. spirit-man (atma).

Such is the inner constitution of the human being, who has, in reality, nine members, although in two cases two of these coincide. Therefore the Rosicrucian method speaks of three times three = nine members, which is reduced to seven because those two pairs coincide. We must, however, recognize the nine within the seven; otherwise we shall reach only a theoretical conception.

The transition from theory to reality can only be made by a study of the human being's essential nature:

9. spirit-man
8. life-spirit
7. spirit-self
6. consciousness soul
5. intellectual soul
4. sentient soul
3. astral body
2. life (ether) body
1. physical body

The 'I' or ego lights up in the soul and then the work on the bodies begins.

We can only make the transition from theory to real life if we look closely at the nature of the situation. The indications given today will be a guide to us tomorrow when we shall study the human being in sleep, in waking consciousness and in death.

Lecture 3

# The Elemental World and the Heaven-World. Waking Life, Sleep and Death

We shall now study the human being in the state of waking life in the physical world, in the state of sleep and in so-called death. From our own experience we are all familiar with the waking state.

When human beings fall asleep, their astral body and ego, together with what has been worked upon in the astral body by the ego, withdraw from the physical and ether bodies. Observing the sleeping human being clairvoyantly you see the physical and ether bodies lying there in bed. These two members remain connected, whereas the astral body withdraws together with the higher members; with clairvoyance we can see how, in a sense, when sleep begins the astral body withdraws from the other two bodies. To describe this condition with greater exactitude we must say that the astral body of the modern human being appears as if it consisted of many streams and sparkles of light, and the whole appears like two intertwining spirals, as if there were two 6-figures, one of which vanishes into the physical body, while the other extends far out into the cosmos like the tail of a comet. Both these tails of the astral body very soon become invisible as they continue to expand, so that the phenomenon then takes on an ovoid shape. When the human being wakes, the tail no longer extends into the cosmos, and everything contracts back again into the ether and physical bodies.

Dreaming is an intermediate condition between waking and sleeping. Sleep that is filled with dreams is a condition in which the astral body has relinquished its connection with the physical body—you could say has withdrawn its feelers from the physical body—but is still connected with the ether body. The human being's field of vision is then pervaded with the pictures we call dreams. This is an intermediate condition because the astral body has detached itself completely from the physical body, while remaining connected in some way with the ether body.

While asleep, human beings live in the astral body outside the physical and ether bodies. The fact that they have to fall asleep has deep significance for their whole make-up. Do not imagine that the astral body is inactive and has no work to do during the night while it is outside the physical and ether bodies. During the day, when the astral body is within the physical and ether bodies, influences come to it from the outside world, impressions which human beings receive as a result of the functioning of their own astral body, through their senses, through their activity in the physical world. Feelings and experiences, everything that works in upon the individual from outside continues on into the astral body. This constitutes the actual feeling and thinking part of the human being; and the physical body, together with what is in the ether body, are only the transmitters, the instruments. The activities of thinking and will take place in the astral body. While the human being is active in the external world during the day, the astral body is receiving impressions all the time. But let us remember, on the other hand, that the astral body is the builder of the ether and physical bodies. Just as the physical body with all its organs has solidified out of the ether body, so everything that streams and is active in the ether body has been born out of the astral body.

Out of what is the astral body itself born? It is born out of the universal astral organism which weaves through the whole of the cosmos that belongs to us. If you want a simile to help you envisage the relation of the small portion of astral substantiality contained in your own astral body to the great astral ocean in which all human beings, animals, plants, minerals, and planets too, are contained and out of which they are born, if you want to envisage the relation of the human astral body to the great astral ocean, think of one drop of a liquid from a glass. The drop derives its existence entirely from the liquid in the glass. Similarly, what is contained in an astral body was once embraced within the astral ocean of the cosmos. It has separated out from this ocean and, having passed into an ether body and a physical body, has become a distinct entity, like the drop taken out of the glass.

As long as the astral body lay within the astral ocean, it received its laws and its impressions from this cosmic astral body. It had its life within this cosmic astral body. After its separation it is exposed, during the individual's waking consciousness, to the impressions received from the physical world; so that it is divided between the influences coming from the cosmic astral body and those which it receives from outside as the result of the activity imposed upon it by the physical world. When humanity has reached the goal of its earth-evolution, this division will merge into harmony. Today, these two kinds of influence do not harmonize.

The astral body is the builder of the ether body and also, indirectly, of the physical body—since the ether body is in turn the builder of the physical body. Everything that the astral body has built up piece by piece, through the ages, has been born out of the great cosmic astral ocean. Because only harmonious and healthy laws proceed from this astral ocean, the work carried out by the astral body in building the ether and physical bodies was originally healthy and harmonious. But as a result of the influences that come to the astral body from outside, from the physical world, impairing its original harmony, there arise all those disturbances of the physical body which prevail in humanity today.

If the astral body were to remain within the human being all the time, the strong influences of the physical world would soon destroy the harmony brought by the astral body from the cosmic ocean. The human being would very soon be spent by illness and exhaustion. During sleep the astral body withdraws from the impressions of the physical world that contain nothing that produces harmony, and passes into the cosmic harmony from which it was born. So in the morning it brings with it the lingering effects of the refreshment and renewal it has experienced during the night. Every night the astral body renews its harmony with the cosmic astral ocean and thus reveals itself to the clairvoyant as anything but inactive. The clairvoyant perceives a connection between the astral ocean and the one comet-like tail, and observes how this part of the astral body works to eliminate the debility caused by the world of disharmony. This activity of the astral body expresses itself in the feeling of refreshed vigour in the morning. Having lived during the night within the great cosmic harmony, the astral body has of course again to adjust itself to the physical world; hence the feeling of greatest vigour does not arise until a few hours have elapsed after waking, when the astral body has again drawn into the physical body.

We will now turn to death, the brother of sleep, and study the condition of the human being after death. The difference between a human being who is dead and one who is only sleeping is that at death the ether body passes away together with the astral body, and the physical body alone is left behind in the physical world. From birth until death the ether body never leaves the physical body except during certain states of initiation.

The period immediately following death is of great importance for the human being. It lasts for many hours, even days, during which the whole of the incarnation that is just over comes before the soul of the dead person as in a great tableau of memories. This happens to every human being after death. The peculiarity of this tableau is that as long as it remains in the form in which it appears immediately after death, all the subjective experiences of the individual during life are as though expunged. Our experiences were always accompanied by feelings either of joy or pain, elation or sorrow. Our outer experience was always associated with an inner life. The joys and sorrows connected with the pictures of the past life are not present in the memory-tableau. The human being confronts this memory-tableau as objectively as he confronts a painting. Even if a painting depicts someone who is sorrowful or full of pain, we still look at it quite objectively. We can, it is true, discern the sorrow, but we do not experience it directly. So it is with these pictures immediately after death. The tableau spreads before us and in an astonishingly brief span of time we see in detail all the events of our life.

Separation of the physical body from the ether body during life can take place only in an initiate, but there are certain moments when the ether body can be suddenly jerked from the physical body. This occurs when someone has a terrifying experience, for example a fall from a high place, or has been in danger of drowning. The shock causes a kind of loosening of the ether body from the physical body, and the consequence is that in such a moment the whole of one's life up to that moment appears before the soul like a memory-picture. This is analogous to the experience after death.

Partial separations of the ether body also occur when a limb has 'gone to sleep', as we say. If a hand, for instance, has gone to sleep, the seer can perceive the etheric part of the hand hanging down like a glove; parts of the etheric brain also hang out when someone is in a state of hypnosis. Because the ether body is woven into the physical body in tiny, pin-point formations, the familiar sensation of pins-and-needles arises in the limb that has gone to sleep.

After the period during which the ether body together with the astral body extricates itself from the physical body after death, there comes the moment when the astral body, in its turn, together with the higher members, extricates itself from the ether body. The latter separates off and the memory-tableau fades away; but something of it remains; it is not wholly lost. What may be called ether or life substance dissipates in the cosmic ether, but a kind of essence remains and this can never be lost to the human being throughout his further journeyings. He bears this within him into all future incarnations as a kind of extract from the life-tableau, even though he has no memory of it. Out of this extract is formed what is called, with concrete reality, the 'causal body'. After every incarnation a new page is added to the Book of Life. This augments the life-essence and, if the past lives were fruitful, causes the next life to develop in a comparable way. This is what causes a life to be rich or poor in talents, qualities and the like.

In order to understand the life of the astral body after its separation from the ether body we must consider the conditions obtaining in physical life. In physical life it is the astral body that is happy, that suffers, that satisfies its desires, impulses and wishes through the organs of the physical body; after death these physical instruments are no longer at its disposal. The epicure can no longer satisfy his desire for choice foods because the tongue has passed away with the physical body; but the desires, being connected with the astral body, remain in the individual, and this gives rise to the 'burning thirst' of the kamaloca period, ('kama' means desire, wish; 'loca' is place, but it is in reality a condition, not a place).

Someone who during physical life learns to transcend the physical body, shortens his time in kamaloca. To take delight in the beauty or harmony of things means growth and development, for this leads us beyond the material world. To delight in art that is materialistic increases the difficulties of the kamaloca state, whereas delight in spiritual art lightens them. Every noble, spiritual delight shortens the time in kamaloca. Therefore already during earthly life we must wean ourselves off pleasures and desires that can be satisfied only by the physical instrument. The period of kamaloca is a time of breaking the habit of material pleasures and impulses. It lasts for approximately one third of the time of an earthly life. There is something singular about the experiences undergone in kamaloca. The individual begins to re-live the whole of his life. Immediately after death the experience was of a memory-picture free of any kind of joy or sorrow. Now, however, all joy and sorrow is re-experienced, but in reverse, so that all the joy or sorrow caused to others is now experienced in oneself. This has nothing to do with the law of karma.

The journey goes backwards, beginning with the last event before death and proceeding at triple speed back to birth. When the human being reaches his birth in his backward journey of remembrance, the part of the astral body that has been transformed by the ego combines with the causal body, and what has not been so transformed falls away like a shadow, a phantom; this is the astral corpse of the human being. He has laid aside the physical corpse and the etheric corpse, and now also the astral corpse. He now lives through new conditions: those of Devachan. Devachan is all around us, just as is the astral world.

When the life has been lived through backwards as far as earliest childhood, when the three corpses have been discarded, the human being reaches the condition mysteriously indicated in the Bible by the words: 'Except ye become as little children, ye cannot enter the kingdom of heaven.' (Devachan, the spiritual world—this is the kingdom of heaven in the Christian sense.)

We must now describe the world of Devachan itself. It is a world as manifold and differentiated as our physical world. Just as solid regions, continents, are distinguished in the physical world, with an expanse of water surrounding firm ground, with the air above, and above the air still more rarefied conditions, so there is a similar differentiation in Devachan, in the spiritual world. By analogy with conditions on earth, the phenomena to be found in Devachan have been given similar names.

Firstly, there is a region that may be compared with firm physical ground: it is the continental region of Devachan. What is physical here on earth is in that region of Devachan a multitude of spiritual beings. Think, for example, of a physical human being. To devachanic vision he appears as follows. What the physical senses perceive, vanishes, and light flashes up in the sphere immediately around the physical human being, where otherwise there is a void; in the middle, where the physical body is, there is an empty, shadowy space—like a kind of negative. Animals and human beings appear here in negative pictures; blood appears green—its complementary colour. All formations that are physical in our world are somehow present in the archetypes of Devachan.

A second region—not separated off, but like a second stage—is the oceanic region of Devachan. It is not water; it is a particular substantiality which in rhythmic streams pervades the world of Devachan in a colour that may be compared with that of new peach-blossom in spring. It is flowing life and it pervades the whole of Devachan. What is distributed among individual human beings and animals here below, is present in Devachan as a kind of watery element. We have a picture of it when we think of the diffusion of the blood in the human organism.

The third region of Devachan can best be characterized by saying that what lives in beings in the physical world by way of feelings, of happiness and suffering, joy, pain and the like, is present there as an external manifestation.

Take an example. Suppose a battle is waged here on the earth. Cannon, weapons and the like—these are all on the physical plane. But within the human beings on the physical plane there are mutual feelings of revenge, pain, passion; the two armies confront one another full of opposing passions. Think of all this translated into external manifestation and you have a picture of how it appears on the devachanic plane. All that happens here on a battlefield appears in Devachan like the breaking out of a fearful thunderstorm. This is the atmosphere, the surrounding air of Devachan. Just as our earth is surrounded by air, so all the feelings that break out here, whether they come to physical expression or not, spread out in Devachan like an atmosphere.

The fourth region of Devachan contains the archetypal forms, the archetypal foundations of all truly original achievements on the earth. If we examine closely the happenings of the physical world, we find that the vast majority of inner processes are instigated from outside. A flower or an animal gives us pleasure; without the flower or the animal we should not experience this particular pleasure. But there are also processes that are not instigated from outside. A new idea, a work of art, a new machine—all these things bring into the world something that was not there before; original creations come into being in all these domains. If new creations did not arise in the world, humanity would make no progress. Creations of exceptional originality given to the world by great artists and discoverers are only a few degrees higher than any other truly original act—even the most insignificant. The point is that something original arises in the inner being.

Archetypes exist in Devachan even for the most insignificant original actions; all these things are already prefigured in that world; any original achievement of a human being is already present there in a germinal state, even before birth.

Thus in Devachan we find four regions whose counter-images on the physical plane are earth, water, air and fire. There is the continental region as the firm crust in Deva-chan—in the spiritual sense, of course; then the oceanic region, corresponding to our area of water; the atmospheric regions, the streaming flow of passions and the like—beauty, but also tumult, is to be found there. Finally, there is the all-pervading world of the archetypes. Everything in the way of initiatives of will and original ideas to which, later on, effect is given in the physical world by beings who return there—all this must be lived through by the soul in that world in order that fresh power may be gathered for the new life.

Lecture 4

# Descent to a New Birth

In the last lecture we described the region and worlds through which human beings have to pass after death, when everything that binds them to their physical instrument has been laid aside in kamaloca or—as one says in Rosicrucian wisdom—the elemental world. We spoke of Rupa-Devachan, or the region known as the heaven-world, the world of Inspiration. We heard that this region—the spirit-land proper—has a fourfold constitution, like the physical world. There is the continental region, permeated by the flowing oceanic region which is more aptly to be compared with the blood circulation in the human organism. In the surrounding 'air' of Devachan, which is analogous to the atmosphere of our earth, is to be found all that pervades the souls of beings in the physical world in the way of joys, sufferings, sorrows, afflictions—only that air must be conceived in a much wider sense because that world is the dwelling-place of other, quite different beings who are not incarnate in physical bodies. Finally we heard how in the fourth region of Devachan everything that is truly original, from the most ordinary idea to the most lofty inspiration of the inventor or artist, exists as an archetype. In that world lies the motive force of the progress of our earth. But in addition to those constituent realms of the spiritual world proper, we find what it is that links our earth with still higher worlds.

Up to now we have been considering things that have reference only to earth-evolution, not those that transcend this evolution. Someone who attains initiation acquires knowledge of what our earth was in the past and will be in the future, of what links the earth with worlds beyond our system.

Important above all in Devachan, in that 'world of reason', is the Akashic Record, as we are accustomed to call it. The Akashic Record is not actually brought into being in Devachan but in an even higher region. However, when the seer has risen to the world of Devachan he can begin to perceive what is known as the Akashic Record.

What is the Akashic Record? We can form the truest conception of it by realizing that whatever comes to pass on our earth makes a lasting impression upon certain delicate essences, an impression which can be discovered by a seer who has attained initiation. It is not an ordinary but a living record. Suppose a human being lived in the first century after Christ; what he thought, felt and willed in those days, what passed into deeds—this is not obliterated but preserved in this delicate essence. The seer can behold it—not as though recorded in a history book, but as it actually happened. How an individual moved, what he did, a journey he took—it can all be seen in those spiritual pictures; the impulses of will, the feelings, the thoughts, can also be seen. But we must not imagine that those pictures are impressions made by physical personalities. That is not the case, as we can see from a simple example. When we move a hand our will pervades the moving hand, and it is this force of will, which is hidden here, that can be seen in the Akashic Record. What is spiritually active in us and has flowed into the physical, is seen there in the spiritual.

Suppose, for example, we look for Caesar. We can follow all his undertakings, but let us be quite clear that it is rather his thoughts that we see in the Akashic Record; when he set out to do something we see the whole sequence of decisions of the will to the point where the deed was actually performed. To observe a specific event in the Akashic Record is not easy. We must help ourselves by linking on to external knowledge. If the seer is trying to observe some action of Caesar and takes an historical date as a point of focus, the result will come more easily. Historical dates are, it is true, often unreliable, but they are sometimes of assistance. Looking for Caesar with the eyes of the seer, we actually see the person of Caesar in action, phantomlike, as though he were there before us, speaking to us. But if someone capable of having a few visions looks into the past, various things might happen to him if he has not entirely found his bearings in the higher worlds.

The Akashic Record is to be found in Devachan, but it extends downwards into the astral world, with the result that in this lower world the pictures of the Akashic Record may often be like a mirage; they are often disconnected and unreliable and it is important to remember this when we set about investigating the past. Let me indicate the danger of these possible mistakes by an example. If the indications of the Akashic Record lead us back to the epoch in the earth's evolution when Atlantis was still in existence, before the great Flood, we can follow the happenings and conditions of life in old Atlantis. These were repeated later on, but in a different form. In northern Germany, in central Europe, eastward of Atlantis, long before the Christian era and long before Christianity made its way there from the South, happenings took place which were a repetition of conditions in Atlantis. Not until after this, through influences coming from the South, did the peoples begin to lead a life that was really their own. Here is an example of how easy it is to be prone to error:

Someone observing the astral pictures of the Akashic Record—not the devachanic pictures—may be confused in regard to these repetitions of Atlantean conditions. This was actually the case in the indications about Atlantis given by Scott-Elliot;[9] they tally with the astral pictures but not with the devachanic pictures of the true Akashic Record. We cannot avoid stating the truth about this matter at some point. The moment we know where the source of the errors lies, it is easy to assess the indications correctly.

Another source of error may arise when reliance is placed upon indications given by mediums. When mediums are possessed of the necessary faculties, they can see the Akashic Record, although in most cases only its reflections in the astral. There is something singular about the Akashic Record. If we discover some person there, he behaves like a living being. If we find Goethe, for example, he may not only answer in the words which he actually spoke in his life but he gives answer in the Goethean sense; he may even utter in his own style verses he never actually wrote. The Akashic picture is so alive that it is like a force working on in the way that human being worked. Hence the picture can become confused with the individuality himself. Mediums believe that they are in contact with the dead person whose life is continuing in the spirit, whereas in reality it is only his Akasha-picture. The spirit of Caesar may already have re-incarnated on earth and it is his Akasha-picture that gives the answers in seances. It is not the individuality of Caesar but only the enduring impression which the picture of Caesar has left behind in the Akashic Record. This is the basis of errors in very many spiritualist seances. We must distinguish between what remains of the human being in his Akasha-picture and what continues to evolve as the true individuality. These are matters of extreme importance.

When human beings have passed out of kamaloca, they have weaned themselves of all the habits for which a physical instrument is necessary. They enter into the region described above. The period that now begins for them is exceedingly important and we must understand what it is that happens.

Everything that they have merely thought or felt, all their passions, confront them in Devachan in the form of things surrounding them. Firstly, they see their own physical body in its archetypal form. Just as here on earth they walk over rocks, mountains and stones, so in Devachan they walk over the archetypes of all the structures that exist in the physical world; thus they also walk over their own physical body there. One characteristic of human beings after death is that their own physical body is an object outside them. This is how they can tell that they have moved up from kamaloka to Devachan. On earth we say to our body: 'This is me.' In Devachan we see our body and say: 'That is you.' Vedantic philosophy teaches its pupils to meditate upon 'That is you' so that through such exercises they may understand what it means to say to the body: 'That is you.'

In Devachan we also see around us all that we have experienced inwardly here on earth. If we have harboured revenge, antipathy or other evil feelings towards our fellow human beings on earth, these confront us from outside like a cloud, and this teaches us what significance and effect all these things have in the world.

Let us be clear about what happens to human beings in Devachan. How have our organs, for example our eyes, been formed? There was a time when no eyes existed yet. The eye has been formed out of the physical organization by light. Light is the progenitor of the eye. What is around us on the earth creates organs in physical bodies and substances; in Devachan what is around us works upon our being of soul. So everything we have developed here on earth in the way of good or reprehensible feelings is to be found in our environment in Devachan; it works upon our soul and thus creates organs of the soul. If we have lived a righteous life on earth, our good qualities live around us in the 'air' of Devachan; they work in the spiritual realm, creating organs. These organs serve as architects and moulders for the building of the physical body in a new incarnation. What was within the human being on earth is transferred to the outer world in Devachan, and prepares the forces that build up the human body for the next birth.

But let it not be imagined that human beings have nothing to do except to care for themselves; in addition to this they have other very important work to do in Devachan. We can form an idea of this if we consider a brief period in the evolution of the earth. How greatly certain regions have changed during the course of a few thousand years! There were once quite different plants, different animal forms, even the climate was different. In respect of the products of nature the earth's surface is continually changing. What once grew on the soil of ancient Greece, for example, could not emerge again now. Evolution proceeds precisely through the fact that the face of the earth undergoes constant change.

When human beings die, a very long period elapses before they are born again, so that when they appear once more on the earth they find quite new conditions. They have to have new experiences; they are not born a second time into the same configuration of the earth. They remain in the spiritual world until the earth has entirely new conditions to offer them. There is good purpose in this, for they thereby learn something entirely new and their development moves forward quite differently. Think of a Roman boy. His life did not in the least resemble that of a modern schoolboy; and when we ourselves are born again we, in turn, shall find quite different conditions. In this way evolution proceeds from incarnation to incarnation. While human beings dwell in the spiritual regions described, the face of the earth is perpetually changing.

What beings are active in this? By what beings are the changes in the earth's physiognomy brought about? This brings us at once to the question: What do human beings do in the period between death and a new birth? They work from the spiritual worlds, under the guidance of higher beings, to transform the earth. It is human beings themselves, between death and rebirth, who carry out this work. When they are born again they find the face of the earth changed, changed into a form which they themselves have helped to fashion. All of us have been engaged in this work.

Where is Devachan; where is the spiritual world? It is around us all the time; it truly is. Around us also are all the souls of discarnate human beings; they are at work around us. While we are building cities and machines, human beings who are living between death and a new birth are around us, working out of the spiritual realms.

When, as seers, we seek for the dead, we can find them within the light—if we perceive the light not merely in a material way. The light that surrounds us forms the 'bodies' of the dead; they have bodies woven out of light. The light that enfolds the earth is 'substance' for the beings who are living in Devachan. A plant nourished by the sunlight receives into itself not the physical light alone but also the activity of spiritual beings, among whom there are also these human souls. These souls themselves ray down upon the plants as light, weaving as spiritual beings around the plants. Looking at the plants with the eye of spirit, we can say: The plant rejoices at the influences coming from the dead who are working and weaving around it in the light. When we observe how the vegetation on the face of the earth changes and ask how this comes about, the answer is: The souls of the dead are at work in the light that envelops the earth; this is where Devachan actually is. After the period of kamaloca we pass into this realm of light. This is a concrete fact. Only those who are able to point to where the dead are actually to be found have any knowledge of Devachan in the sense of Rosicrucian wisdom.

When the faculties of the seer develop, he often makes a striking discovery. As he stands in the sunlight his body impedes the light, so that he casts a shadow. Very often he will discover the spirit for the first time when he looks into this shadow. The body impedes the light, but not the spirit; in the shadow that is cast by the body the spirit can be discovered. That is why more primitive peoples who have always possessed some measure of clairvoyance have also called the soul the 'shadow'; they say 'shadow-less'—'soul-less'. Adelbert Chamisso's novella is unconsciously based on the same idea: the man who has lost his shadow has also lost his soul—hence his despair.[10]

Such, then, is the work that is performed by human beings in Devachan between death and a new birth. They are by no means in a state of inactive repose; they work creatively from Devachan at the evolution of the earth and thus we are able to understand how the world evolves. They are not, as is often said, in a state of blissful rest or dream. Life in Devachan is just as full of activity as life on the earth.

When human beings reach the moment when they have transformed into spiritual forces their activities in their last earthly life, when these experiences have come to them from the outer world of Devachan and have worked upon them, then they are ready to come down from Devachan to a new birth. The earth once more attracts them to its sphere.

The first thing they encounter on their way down from Devachan is the astral region, the elemental world in Rosicrucian terminology. This world gives them their new astral body. If iron filings are scattered on a piece of paper and a magnet is moved about underneath this, the filings arrange themselves into shapes and lines, following the magnetic forces. In exactly the same way, irregularly distributed astral substance is attracted and arranged according to the forces that are in the soul and correspond with what this soul has achieved in the previous life. Thus human beings themselves assemble their astral body. These human beings in the making, who initially have only an astral body, appear to the eye of the seer like bell-shapes opening downwards. They shoot and whirl through the astral world at a tremendous speed—a speed that can hardly be conceived.

These incipient human beings next need to obtain an ether body and a physical body. Up to this point, the stage of the formation of the astral body, the process depended upon themselves, upon the forces they themselves have developed. But the forming of the ether body does not, in the present phase of evolution, depend upon the human being alone. In order to form an ether body, human beings depend upon other beings external to themselves. Consequently although the astral body is always a perfect fit, there is not in every case perfect accordance between astral body and the ether and physical bodies. This is often the cause of disharmony and lack of satisfaction in life. These incipient human beings whirl around space as they do because they are seeking for suitable parents, parents who will afford them the best opportunity of receiving an ether and a physical nature that fits their astral being. The parents who provide this can only be relatively the best and most suitable. Cooperating in this search are beings who attach the ether body to the astral body and who are similar to those often called folk-spirits. Such spirits are not the intangible abstraction they are usually considered to be. A folk-spirit is as real to the eye of the seer as our soul that is incarnate in our body. A whole people, although it does not have a common physical body, has a common astral body and rudiments of a common ether body. The people as a whole lives within a kind of astral cloud, and this is the 'body' of the folk-spirit. Such bodies guide the ether-formations around the human being, who is thus no longer entirely under his own control.

Now comes a moment of extreme importance, equally as important as the moment after death when the whole of the past life is seen as a memory-picture. When human beings pass into their ether body but have not yet acquired their

physical body—it is a brief moment, but of supreme importance—they have a prevision of their coming life, not in all its
details but only as a survey over what this future life has in
store for them. Although they forget this at the moment of
physical incorporation, they can realize that they are about to
embark on a happy or an unhappy life. If an individual has had
many unfortunate experiences in the previous life, it may now
happen that he gets a shock and is hesitant to enter into the
physical body. The result of this may be that he does not come
right down into the physical body and so the connection
between the various bodies is not fully established. This can
produce idiocy in the coming life; it is not always the cause of
idiocy, but frequently it is so. It is as though the soul were
resisting incarnation into the physical body. Such a human
being cannot make proper use of his brain because he is not
correctly incarnated in it. He can only use his physical
instrument aright when he allows himself to be born into it in
the full and proper sense. Whereas in other circumstances the
ether body extends only slightly beyond the physical, in the
case of idiocy portions of the ether body are often to be seen as
an etheric sheen extending far beyond the head. Here is a case
where something that is left unexplained by physical observation of life can be explained through spiritual science.

# Communal Life between Death and a New Birth into the Physical World

We have come to the point in our studies where we heard that the human being who is descending from spiritual regions is clothed in an ether body and has, for a brief moment, a prevision of the life that is awaiting him on earth. We saw the abnormalities and conditions to which this may give rise. Before proceeding, we will answer a question that may seem of importance to those who turn their spiritual eyes to Devachan: In what sense is there community of life among human beings between death and a new birth? There is indeed community of life not only among people on the physical earth but also in the higher worlds. Just as the activities of human beings in the spirit-realm reach down into the physical world, so do all the relationships and connections that are established between individuals on earth stretch up into the spiritual world.

We will take a concrete example of this, namely the relationship between mother and child. Is there a relationship between them that endures? There is indeed, and moreover a much more intimate, much firmer relationship than can ever be established here on earth. At first mother-love is a kind of natural instinct, it has something of an animal character. As the child grows up this relationship becomes a moral, ethical, spiritual one. When mother and child learn to think together, when they share experiences in common, natural instinct withdraws more and more into the background; it has merely provided the opportunity for the forging of that beautiful bond which is present in the very highest sense in the mother's love for the child and the child's love for the mother. The mutual understanding and love that unfolds here continues on into the regions of the spiritual world even though, as the result of the one dying earlier, the other seems for a time to be separated from the dead. After this period has passed, the link that was on earth is equally vital and intimate. The two are together, only all the purely natural, animal instincts must have been laid aside. The feelings and thoughts that weave between one soul and another on earth are not hindered in the spiritual world by the barriers that exist on earth. Devachan actually assumes a particular appearance and structure as a result of the relationships that are woven here on earth.

Let us take another example. Friendships and affinities are born from the kinship of souls; they continue on into Devachan, and from them the social connections for the next life develop. By establishing connections with souls here, we are therefore working at the form which Devachan acquires. We have all of us worked in this way when bonds of love were forged between ourselves and others; thereby we create something that has significance not only for the earth but which also shapes conditions in Devachan. What happens here as the fruit of love, of friendship, of mutual understanding—all these things are building-stones of temples in the spiritual region above, and those who have this certainty cannot but be inspired by the knowledge that when bonds are forged from soul to soul here on earth, this is the foundation of an eternal becoming.

Let us suppose for a moment that on some other physical planet there were beings incapable of mutual sympathy, incapable of forming bonds of love amongst one another. Such beings would have a very barren Devachan. Only a planetary region where bonds of love are forged between one being and another can have a Devachan rich in content and variety. Although his presence cannot be experienced by ordinary humans, someone who is already in Devachan possesses greater or less consciousness of communion with those who have remained behind on the earth, depending on his stage of development. There are even means whereby these bonds of communion can be intensified. If we send thoughts of love—but not of egoistic love—to the dead, we strengthen the sense of community with them.

It is a mistake to assume that the consciousness of the human being in Devachan is dim or shadowy. This is not the case. The degree of consciousness once attained by an individual can never be lost, although darkenings can occur during certain periods of transition. Human beings in Devachan have, through their spiritual organs, clear consciousness of what is happening in the sphere of the earth. Esotericism reveals that human beings in the spiritual world share an experience of what is taking place on the earth.

So we see that life in Devachan, if viewed in its reality, loses every element of comfortlessness. We see that human beings, when they cease to regard it from their earthly, egoistic standpoint, can experience it as a condition of infinite blessedness—quite apart from the fact that any freedom from the physical body, freedom from the lower nature in which they are enclosed here, brings with it a feeling of intense relief anyway. The fact that the barriers have fallen away—this in itself brings a feeling of rapture. Devachan is thus a time of expansion and expression in all directions; there is a richness and an absence of restriction that are never experienced on the earth.

We have heard that on their descent to a new birth, human beings are clothed with a new ether body by beings of a rank similar to that of the folk-spirits. This ether body is not a perfect fit for the reincarnating individual, and still less perfectly fitted is the physical body he receives. We will now speak in broad outline of the incorporation of human beings into the physical world. Something more detailed would in some ways be unsuitable for public description.

We have heard that in accordance with their qualities, human beings clothe themselves with an astral body. Through what is contained in this astral body they are attracted to certain human beings here on the earth, and through the ether body they are drawn to the nation, and to the family in the wider sense, into which they are to be born anew. According to the way in which they have developed their astral body, they are drawn to the mother; the essence, the substance, the organization of the astral body draws them to the mother. The ego draws them to the father. The ego was present even in ages of remote antiquity, when the soul descended for the first time from the depths of the Godhead into an earthly body. This ego has developed through many incarnations. The ego, the 'I', of one human being is distinct from the ego of another, and at the present stage of evolution gives rise to the force of attraction to the father. The ether body attracts human beings to the nation, to the family; the astral body attracts them particularly to the mother, and the 'I' to the father. The whole descent to the new incarnation is guided in accordance with these principles.

It may happen that the astral body is attracted to a mother but that the ego is not attracted to the corresponding father; in such a case the search continues until a suitable pair of parents is found.

In the present phase of evolution, the 'I' or ego represents the element of will, of impulses of sensitivity. In the astral body lie the capacities of fancy or imagination, the capacities of thinking. The latter qualities, therefore, are transmitted by the mother, the former by the father. The individuality who is approaching incarnation uses unconscious forces to seek out the parents who are to provide the physical body.

In its essentials, all this takes place by about the third week after conception. From the moment of conception onwards the being consisting of 'I', astral and ether bodies remains near the mother who carries the fertilized human ovum, working on it from the outside. Then, at about the third week, the astral and ether bodies take hold, you might say, of the ovum and now begin to participate in the work on the embryo. Up to that moment the development of the physical body proceeds without influence of the astral and ether bodies, but from then onwards these bodies participate in the development of the child and themselves influence the further development of the embryo. We thus see that what was said about the ether body holds good still more for the physical body, so that complete suitability is even less easy to obtain here. This significant fact sheds light upon a great deal that happens in the world.

Up to this point we have been speaking of the normal evolution of the average modern human being. What has been said does not altogether hold good of someone in whom spiritual development began in a previous incarnation. The higher the stage attained then, the earlier does such an individual begin to work upon his own physical body in order to make it more suitable for the mission to be fulfilled on earth this time. The later the individual takes command of the physical ovum, the less control will he have over the physical body. The most highly developed individualities, those who are the guides and leaders of the spiritual life of the earth, take command even at the moment of conception. Nothing takes place without their collaboration; they direct their physical body right up to the time of their death and begin to prepare a new body directly the first impetus for this is given.

The substances of which the physical body is composed are perpetually changing; after about seven years, every particle has been renewed. The substance is exchanged, but the form endures. Between birth and death the substances of the physical body must continually be born anew; they are the ever-changing element. What we develop between birth and death in such a way that death has no power over it, this is preserved and builds up a new organism.

The initiate performs consciously, between death and a new birth, what the average human being performs unconsciously between birth and death; the initiate consciously builds up his new physical body. For him, therefore, birth amounts to no more than an outstanding event in his existence. He exchanges the substances only once, but then fundamentally. Hence there is considerable similarity of stature and form in such individualities from one incarnation to the next, whereas in those who are but little developed there is no similarity of form whatever in their successive incarnations. The higher the development of a human being, the greater is the similarity in two successive incarnations; this is clearly perceptible to clairvoyant sight. There is a specific expression to describe this higher stage of development; it is not said that such an individual is born in a different body any more than it is said of the average human being that he receives a new body every seven years. Of a Master it is said: He is born in the same body; he uses it for hundreds, even thousands of years. This is the case with the vast majority of leading individualities. An exception is formed by certain Masters who have their own special mission; with them the physical body remains, so that death does not occur for them at all. These are the Masters whose task it is to watch over and bring about the transition from one root-race or epoch to another.

Two other questions arise at this point, that of the duration of the sojourn in the spiritual worlds, and that of the individual's gender in consecutive incarnations.

Esoteric investigation reveals that 1,000 to 1,300 years is

the average span of time between incarnations. The reason for this is that the individual will find the face of the earth changed on his or her return and therefore be able to have new experiences. Changes on the earth are closely connected with certain constellations of the stars. This is a very significant fact. At the beginning of spring the sun rises in a certain zodiacal constellation. It began to rise in Aries 800 years before Christ. Before that epoch it rose in the adjacent constellation of Taurus. About 2,160 years are required for the passage through one constellation. The circuit through the whole twelve constellations is known in esotericism as a cosmic year.

The peoples of antiquity were deeply sensible of what is connected with this passage through the zodiac. With feelings of awe and reverence they said: When the sun rises in spring, nature is renewed after its winter repose; nature is awakened from deep sleep by the divine rays of the vernal sun. This young, fresh power of spring linked itself with the constellation from which the sun was shining. They said: This constellation is the bestower of the sun with its new vigour, it is the bestower of the new, divinely creative power. Thus the Lamb was regarded as the benefactor of humanity by those living 2,000 years ago. All sagas and legends concerning the Lamb originated during that age. Conceptions of the Godhead were associated with this symbol. During the early centuries of our era, the Redeemer himself, Christ Jesus, was depicted by the symbol of the Cross and beneath it the Lamb. Not until the sixth century AD was the Redeemer portrayed on the Cross. The sun rising in Aries is, similarly, also the origin of the well-known myth of Jason and the quest of the Golden Fleece.

In the epoch preceding 800BC the sun was passing through the constellation of Taurus; in Egypt we find the veneration of the Apis bull, in Persia the veneration of the

Mithras bull. Earlier still, the sun was passing through the constellation of Gemini. In Indian and Germanic mythologies we find definite indications of twins, the twin he-goats drawing the chariot of the god Donar are a last remnant of this. Finally we reach back to the epoch of Cancer which brings us near to the time of the Atlantean Flood. An ancient culture passed away and a new culture arose. This was designated by a particular esoteric sign, the vortex, which is the symbol of Cancer and is to be found in every calendar.

Thus peoples have always had a clear consciousness of the fact that what proceeds in the heavens runs parallel with the changes taking place on the earth beneath. When the sun has completed its passage through one constellation, the face of the earth has changed to such an extent that it is profitable for the human being to enter a new life. For this reason the time of reincarnation depends upon the precession of the vernal equinox. The period required by the sun for its passage through one zodiacal constellation is the period within which the human being is twice incarnated, once as a man and once as a woman. The experiences in a male and female organism are so fundamentally different for spiritual life that the human being incarnates once as a woman and once as a man into the same conditions of the earth. This makes an average of 1,000 to 1,300 years between two incarnations.

Here we have the answer to the question concerning gender. As a rule, gender alternates. This rule, however, is often broken, so that sometimes there are three to five, but never more than seven consecutive incarnations in the same gender. To say that seven consecutive incarnations in the same gender are the rule, contradicts all esoteric experience.

Before we begin to study the karma of the individual human being, one fundamental fact must be borne in mind. There is a common karma, a karma that is not determined by the single individual although it is adjusted in the course of that individual's incarnations. Here is a concrete example:

When the Huns poured over from Asia into the countries of Europe during the early Middle Ages, causing alarming wars, there was a significant spiritual aspect to this. The Huns were the last surviving remnants of ancient Atlantean peoples; they were in an advanced stage of decadence which expressed itself in a certain process of decay in their astral and ether bodies. These products of decay found good soil in the fear and terror the Huns caused among the peoples. The result was that these products of decay were inoculated into the astral bodies of the peoples and in a later generation this was carried over into their physical bodies. The skin absorbed the astral elements and the outcome was a disease prevalent in the Middle Ages: leprosy. An ordinary doctor would of course attribute leprosy to physical causes. I have no wish to dispute what such doctors say, but their line of reasoning is as follows: In a fight, someone wounds another with a knife; he has harboured an old feeling of revenge against him. One person will say that the cause of the wound was the feeling of revenge, another that the knife was the cause. Both are right. The knife was the final physical cause, but behind it there is the spiritual cause. Those who seek for spiritual causes will always also admit the validity of physical causes.

We see that historical events have a significant effect upon whole generations and we learn how, even in such fundamental conditions as health, we can bring about improvements over long periods of time.

As a result of technical progress in recent centuries an industrial proletariat has developed among the peoples of Europe, and together with it, untold rank and class hatred.[11] This has its seat in the astral body and comes to physical expression as pulmonary tuberculosis. Such knowledge is revealed by spiritual research. It is often not within our power to help those who are afflicted by general karma of this kind. We are often compelled, with aching hearts, to see an individual suffering without being able to make him well or happy because he is caught in the network of general karma. Only by working for the improvement of the common karma can we also help the individual. It should not be our aim to promote the well-being of the single, egotistic self, but to work in such a way that we serve the well-being of humanity as a whole.

Another example, directly connected with current events, is the following. Spiritual observations have revealed that among the astral beings who participated in the various battles of the Russo-Japanese war there were dead Russians, working against their own people.[12] This was due to the fact that during recent times in the development of the Russian people, many noble idealists perished in the dungeon or on the scaffold. They were men of high ideals, but they were not so far developed as to be able to forgive. They died with feelings of bitter revenge against those who had been the cause of their death. These feelings of revenge were lived out in their kamaloca period, for only in kamaloca is this possible. From the astral plane after their death, they filled the souls of the Japanese soldiers with hatred and revenge against the people to whom they themselves had belonged. Had they already been in Devachan, they would have said: I forgive my enemies! For in Devachan, with the clouds of hatred and revenge confronting them from without, they would have realized how terrible and how unworthy such feelings are. Thus spiritual investigation reveals that whole peoples fall under the influence of their forefathers.

The idealistic endeavours of modern times cannot attain their goals because people are willing to work only with physical means on the physical plane. This applies, for example, to the Society for the Promotion of Peace, which sets out to bring about peace by physical methods alone. Not until we learn how to influence the astral plane too can we recognize the right methods; not until then can we work in such a way that when the human being is born again he will find a world in which he can labour fruitfully.

# Lecture 6

# The Law of Destiny

Today we come to the human being's experiences in the physical world, in so far as these are determined by an earlier incarnation. At the outset it must be emphasized that life is not determined by previous incarnations alone but also, though in small degree, by the current life. The law according to which the human being's past, present and future are linked is called in spiritual science the law of karma. It is the true law of human destiny; an individual life is only a specific application of the great law of the cosmos, for the law of karma is a universal, cosmic law of which human life is merely a specific application. Whenever we envisage a connection between preceding conditions and subsequent effects, we are thinking in line with this law. I want therefore to explain in detail the individual application of this cosmic law in the life of the human being.

Suppose we have two vessels of water and put into one of the vessels a red-hot iron ball. The water will splutter and become warm. If we take the ball out and put it into the other vessel, the water in this case will neither splutter nor get warm, because the ball is no longer red-hot; it has been cooled by immersion in the first vessel of water. The effect of the behaviour of the iron ball in the first vessel determines its behaviour in the second. Thus are cause and effect always connected in physical life. Subsequent behaviour always depends on what has happened previously.

Another example is afforded by certain animals whose organs of sight have atrophied in consequence of their having migrated into dark holes or caves. In such animals, the substances which formerly nourished the eyes are sent to other parts of the body, because as it is no longer necessary for the eyes to see, these substances are not required. The eyes have atrophied and will remain atrophied in all subsequent generations. Through their earlier migrations these animals determined the behaviour of their organs; the destiny of subsequent generations was determined by what had happened in the past. These animals prepared their destiny for the future.

The same goes for human life. Human beings determine their future by their past, and because their innermost being is not confined to one incarnation but passes through many, the causes of what confronts them in a given life are to be sought in an earlier life.

We will now consider the chain of events that becomes comprehensible if we think of the consequences of human deeds, thoughts and feelings. It is often said in everyday life: Thoughts don't cost anything!—meaning that we can think what we like and nobody in the external world will be affected. This is one important point where someone who has really grasped spiritual impulses is at variance with the materialistic thinker.

The materialist agrees that injury is caused if he throws a stone at somebody, but he thinks that a thought of hatred which he may harbour against a fellow human being does not hurt him. However, those who have real knowledge of the world know that far, far stronger effects proceed from a thought filled with hatred than can ever be caused by a stone. Everything we think and feel has its effects in the astral world, and the seer can follow with great precision the effect of a loving thought that goes out to someone, and the very different effect that is produced by a thought filled with hatred. When you send out a loving thought to someone, the seer perceives a form of light, shaped like a sort of flower-calyx, playing lovingly around that person's ether and astral bodies, thereby contributing something to his vitality and happiness. On the other hand, a thought of hatred bores its way into the ether and astral bodies like a wounding arrow.

Very varied observations are to be made in this domain. There is a tremendous difference in the astral world if someone voices a thought that is true or one that is untrue. A thought is related to a specific thing and is true if it coincides with that thing. Every event that happens causes an effect in the higher worlds. If someone relates this event truly, an astral form rays out from the teller, unites with the form emanating from the event itself, and both are strengthened. These strengthened forms help to make our spiritual world richer and more full of content—which is necessary if humanity is to make progress. But if the event is related untruthfully, in a way that does not coincide with the facts, then the thought-form of the teller comes up against the thought-form that has proceeded from the event; the two thought-forms collide, causing mutual destruction. These destructive 'explosions' caused by lies work in the way a tumour works in the body, destroying the organism. Thus lies kill the astral forms that have arisen and must arise, and in this way they obstruct or paralyse a part of evolution. Everyone who tells the truth actually promotes the evolution of humanity, and everyone who lies obstructs it. Therefore there is this esoteric law: Seen with the eyes of spirit, a lie is a murder. Not only does it kill an astral form, but it is also kills the self. Anyone who lies places obstacles along his own path. Such effects are to be observed everywhere in the spiritual world. The clairvoyant sees that everything a person thinks, feels and experiences has its effect in the astral world.

An individual's disposition, temperament, enduring qualities of character, thoughts that are not merely transient—all this streams continually not only into the astral world but into

the world of Devachan as well. Someone with a happy disposition is a source, a centre, of certain processes in Devachan; someone who is mournful has the effect of multiplying
the essences and substances associated with mournfulness in
the human character. Thus spiritual science shows us that we
do not live as isolated beings but that our thoughts continually
produce forms which cause shades of differing intensity in the
world of Devachan and fill it with all kinds of substances and
essences. The four regions of Devachan—the continental, the
oceanic, the atmospheric, and the region of original inspira-
tions—are influenced all the time by the thoughts, feelings
and sensations of human beings. The higher regions of
Devachan, in which the Akashic Record plays a part, are
influenced by deeds. What happens in the external world
plays into the very highest region of Devachan—the one we
have designated the 'world of reason'.

We shall understand in this way how on descending to a
new incarnation the human being reconstitutes his astral body
and attaches it to himself. All his thoughts, feelings and
experiences had become integral parts of the astral world,
leaving many traces there. If his thoughts contained much
truth, these traces would gather together to form a good astral
body for him. What he has incorporated into the lower
Devachanic world as his temperament and so on, gathers
together the new ether body, and from the highest regions of
Devachan where the Akashic Record is to be found, his past
deeds play their part in establishing the siting, the localization
of the physical body. Here lie the forces that bring a human
being to a definite locality. If a person has done evil to
someone, this is an external fact that reaches into the highest
regions of Devachan; when the time comes to enter a new
physical body it works as forces that the person has left in his
wake, and impels him—under the guidance of higher
beings—to the associations and the place where he will now

be able to experience the effects of his past deeds in the physical world.

Experiences in the external world that do not inwardly affect us very strongly work upon our astral body in the next incarnation, drawing into it corresponding feelings and a characteristic life of thought. If a person has spent his life profitably, if he has been very observant and has acquired wide knowledge, his astral body in the next incarnation will be born with special gifts in these directions. Experience and acquired knowledge thus express themselves, in the next incarnation, in the astral body. Inner experience, all that a person feels in the way of happiness, sorrow and so on—this works down to the ether body in the next incarnation and imbues it with lasting propensities. The ether body of someone who experiences much happiness will have a temperament disposed to joy. Someone who tries to perform many good deeds will, as a result of the feelings evoked, have a decided talent in the next life for good deeds; he will also possess a thoroughly developed conscience and will be a person of high moral principles.

Everything carried by the ether body in the present life—the permanent character, talents, etc.—appears in the next life in the physical body. For instance, someone who has developed bad inclinations and passions in one life will be born in the next with an unhealthy physical body. Conversely, a person who enjoys good health, and has great powers of endurance, unfolded good qualities in the previous life. A person who is continually prone to illness has worked bad impulses into himself. Thus we have it in our power to create for ourselves health or illness in so far as these inhere in the natural constitution of the physical body. All that is required is the elimination of bad tendencies for we then prepare a healthy, vigorous physical body for the next life.

It is possible to observe, in all details, how the tendencies that were present in one life work, in the next, on the physical body. A person who is disposed to love everything around him, who is loving to all creatures, who pours out love, will have in the next incarnation a physical body that remains young and fresh until late in life. Love for all beings, the cultivation of sympathy, gives rise to a physical body that preserves its youthful vigour. Someone who is full of antipathy against other human beings, who criticizes and grumbles at everything, trying to keep aloof from it all, produces as a result of these tendencies a physical body that ages and becomes wrinkled prematurely. In this way the tendencies and passions of one life are carried over to the physical, bodily life of the subsequent incarnation.

This can be observed in every detail, so that we can see how a passion for acquisition, an urge that makes a person hoard possessions and becomes a rooted disposition in him, pro-duces, in the next life, a tendency to infectious diseases in the physical body. It is perfectly possible to confirm cases where a pronounced tendency to infectious diseases leads back to an earlier, very strong sense of acquisition, the bearer of this quality being the ether body. On the other hand impartial endeavour, free from any desire for self-profit and wishing only to work for the well-being of all humanity—this tendency in the ether body gives rise, in the next life, to a strong power of resistance to infectious diseases.

Thus knowledge of the connection between the physical and astral worlds enables us to have a clear understanding of the world in its inner process of evolution; things are often connected in quite a different way from the one people like to imagine. Many people complain about pain and suffering, but from a higher point of view this is quite unjustified, for if they can be overcome, then, when the person is ready for a new incarnation, suffering and pain are the sources of wisdom, prudence and comprehensiveness of vision. Even in a modern work written from the materialistic standpoint, we find it stated that there is something like 'crystallized pain' in the physiognomy of every thinker. What this materialistically-minded author says here has long been known to the spiritual researcher, for the greatest wisdom of the world is acquired by the quiet endurance of pain and suffering; this creates wisdom in the next incarnation.

No one who shudders at the unpleasantness of pain, who is unwilling to bear pain, can create in himself the foundations for wisdom. Indeed, when we look deeper we cannot really bemoan illnesses, for regarded from a higher standpoint, from the standpoint of eternity, they take on a very different aspect. Illnesses calmly borne often appear in the next life as great physical beauty; great physical beauty in a human being is acquired at the cost of illness in a preceding life. Such is the connection between impairment of the body through illness, particularly also through external circumstances, and beauty.

The words of the French writer, Fabre d'Olivet, can be applied to this very remarkable connection:[13] When we observe the life of the human being, it often seems to be like the formation of the pearl in the oyster-shell—the pearl can only come into being through disease. This is exactly the case in human life. Beauty is karmically connected with illnesses and is their result. When I said, however, that someone who unfolds reprehensible passions creates in himself the disposition to illness, it must be fully understood that in this case it is a matter of an inherent tendency to illnesses. It is a different matter when someone falls ill through working in a poisonous atmosphere; that, too, may be a cause of illness, but is not connected with the inherent constitution of the physical body.

Everything that is a fact on the physical plane, everything that constitutes a deed, expressing itself in such a way that it has a definite effect in the physical world, from a footstep or movement of the hand to the most complicated processes, for instance the building of a house, comes to the human being in a later incarnation from the outside as an actual physical effect. As you see, we live our life from within outwards. What lives as joy, pain, happiness, sorrow in the astral body appears again in the ether body; the lasting impulses and passions that are rooted in the ether body appear in the physical body as constitutional tendencies; deeds that require the agency of the physical body appear as outer destiny in the next incarnation. What the astral body does becomes the destiny of the ether body; what the ether body does becomes the destiny of the physical body; and what the physical body does comes back from outside in the next incarnation as a physical reality.

Here you have the actual point where external destiny intervenes in human life. This working of destiny may be postponed for a long time but must inevitably approach the human being sooner or later. If a human being's life is fol-lowed through the different incarnations, it can always be seen that life in a subsequent incarnation is prepared by beings who work at his physical embodiment in such a way that he is led to a particular place in order that his destiny may overtake him.

Here again is an example drawn from life. At a Vehmic court in the Middle Ages a number of judges condemned a man to death and executed the sentence themselves. Earlier incarnations of the judges and of the executed man were investigated and it was found that they had all been con-temporaries; the prisoner who had been put to death had been the chief of a tribe who had ordered the death of those who were now the Vehmic judges. The deed of the former physical life had created the connection between the persons, and the forces had inscribed themselves in the Akashic Record. When a person again comes down to incarnation, these forces cause him to be born at the same time and place as those to whom he is tied in this way, and they work out his destiny. The

Akashic Record is a veritable source of power in which everything that is due to be expiated between one human being and another is inscribed. Some people can sense these processes, but very, very few are really conscious of them.

Suppose someone has a profession in which he is apparently happy and contented; for some reason or other he is forced to leave it and, finding no other occupation in the same place, is driven far away—into another country, where he has to strike out on an entirely new line of work. Here he finds a person with whom he has in some way to be associated. What has happened in such a case? He once lived with the person whom he has now met, and remained in his debt for some reason or other. This is inscribed in the Akashic Record and the forces have led him to this place in order that he may meet the person and discharge his debt.

Between birth and death the human being is perpetually within a network of these forces of soul which weave around him on all sides; they are the directing powers of his life. You bear within you all the time the workings of earlier lives; and all the time you are experiencing the outcome of former incarnations.

You will realize, therefore, that your lives are guided by powers of which you yourself are not aware. The ether body is worked upon by forms that you yourself previously called into existence on the astral plane; beings and forces in the higher regions of Devachan, inscribed by you in the Akashic Record, work upon your destiny. These forces or beings are not unknown to the spiritual researcher; they have their own place in the ranks of similar beings. You must realize that in your astral body and in your ether body, as well as in your physical body, you feel the workings of other beings. All that you do involuntarily, everything to which you are impelled, is due to the working of other beings; it is not born from nothingness. The various members of the human being are all the time actually permeated and filled by other beings, and many of the exercises given by an initiated teacher are for the purpose of driving out these beings in order that an individual may become more and more free.

The beings who permeate the astral body and make it unfree are known as 'demons'. Your astral body is always interpenetrated by demons, and the beings you yourself generate through your true or false thoughts are of such a nature that they gradually grow into demons. There are good demons, generated by good thoughts; but bad thoughts, above all those that are untruthful, generate demoniacal forms of the most terrible and frightful kind, and these interlard the astral body—if I may so express it. The ether body is also permeated by beings from which human beings must free themselves; these beings are called 'spectres', 'ghosts'. Finally, permeating the physical body there are beings known as 'phantoms'. Besides these three classes there are yet other beings, the 'spirits', who drive the ego hither and thither—the ego itself also being a spirit. It is a fact that you generate such beings who then determine your inner and outer destiny when you descend to incarnation. These beings work in your life in such a way that you can feel the 'demons' created by your astral body, the 'ghosts' or 'spectres' created by your ether body, and the 'phantoms' created by your physical body. All these beings are related to you and approach you when the time comes for reincarnation.

It can be seen how religious scriptures express these truths. When the Bible tells of the driving-out of demons, this is not an abstraction but is to be taken literally. Christ Jesus healed those who were possessed by demons; he drove the demons out of the astral body. This is an actual process and the passage is to be taken literally. The wise man Socrates also spoke of his 'daimon' which worked in his astral body. This was a good demon; such beings are not always evil.

There are, however, terrible and corrupt demonic beings. All demons that are born of lying work in such a way as to cause the human being to regress in his development; and because, owing to the lies of eminent figures in world-history, demons who grow into very powerful beings are all the time being created, we hear of the 'spirits of hindrance', the 'spirits of obstruction'. In this sense Faust calls Mephistopheles: 'The father, thou, of all impediments!'[14]

The individual human being, integrated as he is within humanity as a whole, has an effect upon the whole world according to whether he speaks the truth or lies; beings created by truth or by lies produce quite different effects. Imagine a people that is composed entirely of liars; the astral plane would be populated solely by the corresponding demons, and those demons would be able to express themselves in a constitutional tendency to epidemics. Thus certain types of bacillus are bearers of infectious diseases; they stem from the lies told by human beings; they are nothing other than physically embodied demons generated by lies.

Lies and untruths of earlier ages appear in world-karma as a definite cohort of beings. A passage in *Faust* indicates how much deep truth is contained in myths and sagas. You will find there a connection between vermin and lies and also the role of rats and mice in connection with Mephistopheles, the lying spirit.[15] Legends have often preserved wonderful indications of the connection between the spiritual world and the physical world.

In order to understand the law of karma we shall have to speak about many other things. Spiritual science as a movement is itself the outcome of an intimate knowledge of the law of karma.

You have just heard that forces which exist in the ether body work upon the physical body in the next incarnation. Thus the attitude of mind, the tendency to think in a specific manner, works upon the physical body. A spiritual or a materialistic attitude of mind is by no means without importance for the next incarnation. An individual who has some knowledge of the higher worlds—he need only believe in their existence—has in his next life a well-centred physical body and tranquil nervous system, a body which he has well in hand, including even the nerves. On the other hand, an individual who believes in nothing except what is to be found in the world of the senses, communicates this kind of thinking to his physical body and in the next incarnation has a body prone to nervous disorders, a frail, fidgety body in which there is no steadfast centre of will. The materialist disintegrates into many separate fragments; the spirit binds together, for spirit is unity.

In the individual, this tendency appears in his next incarnation, but it also continues through the generations, so that the children and grandchildren of materialistic fathers have to pay for this by badly constituted nervous systems and nervous disorders. A nervous era such as ours is the outcome of the materialistic attitude of the last century. To counteract this, the great teachers of humanity have recognized the necessity of allowing the inflow of spiritual ways of thinking.

Materialism has even found its way into religion. There are people who believe in the spiritual worlds but have not the will to acquire real knowledge of them. Can it be said that such people are not materialists? It is materialism in religion that makes people want to have the mystery of the six days of creation—as the Bible describes the evolution of the cosmos—displayed before their eyes; it is materialism that speaks of Christ Jesus as an historical personality and ignores the Mystery of Golgotha. Materialism in science is primarily a consequence of materialism in religion; it would not exist if the religious life were not saturated with materialism. People who have been too lazy to deepen their religious life are the ones who have introduced materialism into science. The derangement of the nerves caused by this materialism works itself out among whole peoples and nations, as well as in the individual.

If the stream of spirituality is not powerful enough to influence lazy and easy-going people as well, then nervous disorder, the karmic consequence, will gain greater and greater hold over humanity; and just as in the Middle Ages there were epidemics of leprosy, so, in future, materialistic thinking will give rise to grave nervous diseases—epidemics of insanity will beset whole nations.

Insight into this domain of the law of karma should not make spiritual science a matter of strife but a healing power in humanity. The more spiritual human beings become, the more will troubles connected with disorders of the nervous system and derangement in the life of soul be eliminated.

# The Technique of Karma

To help you understand how the law of karma works in human life, I shall speak of something that happens immediately after the death of a human being. We heard of the memory-tableau that appears when he is freed from his physical body and lives for a short time in the ether and astral bodies before passing through the elemental world.

To show you the inner working of karma, let me describe a strange feeling that arises during the experience of this great tableau. It is a feeling of expansion, of growing beyond oneself. This feeling becomes stronger and stronger as long as we are still living in our ether body. We have a strange experience in connection with this tableau. First of all we see pictures of our past life as in a panorama. Then a moment comes, not very long after death and lasting for hours, even days, according to the nature of the individual, when we feel: I myself am all these pictures. We feel our ether body growing and expanding as if it embraced the whole surrounding sphere of the earth as far as the sun.

Then, when the ether body has been abandoned, another very remarkable feeling arises, one that is really difficult to describe in words drawn from the physical world. It is a feeling of expansion into wide cosmic space but as though one did not actually fill out every place in it. The experience can only be approximately described. The individual feels as though with one part of his being he were in Munich, with another part in Mainz, a third in Basle, and another far outside the earth sphere, perhaps on the moon. He feels as though he were dismembered, as though he were not connected with the spaces in between. This is the specific way in which one experiences oneself as an astral being, spread out in space, transferred to different centres, but not filling the regions between them.

This experience lasts throughout the kamaloca period during which we live through our life backwards to birth. We live through all that belongs to us and these experiences then become part of the rest of life in kamaloca. It is important to know this in order to picture how the law of karma works. The individual feels, at the beginning, as though he were within that human being with whom he was last connected and then, retrogessively, within all the persons and other beings with whom he was associated during his life.

Suppose, for example, you once thrashed someone in Mainz. After your death, when the time comes, you experience the thrashing you gave, with its accompanying pain. If that person is still in Mainz, a part of your astral body after your death feels itself in Mainz, experiencing the event there. If the person you thrashed has died in the meantime, you feel yourself at the place in kamaloca where he now is. You have, of course, been connected not only with one but with many human beings who are scattered over the earth and in kamaloca. You are everywhere and this gives rise to the feeling of dismemberment of the bodily nature in kamaloca. It is thereby possible for you to experience in all the others the associations you had with them, and you thus form a lasting connection with everyone with whom you have come into contact. You have a tie with this individual whom you thrashed because you have lived with him in kamaloca. Later on you pass into Devachan and then, in turn, back through kamaloca. During the process of building a new body, your astral body once again finds the ties which bind it to the person with whom you were united. And since there are many such connections you find that you are linked by a kind of bond with everything with which you were associated.

The event observed by spiritual sight, of which I told you in the last lecture, offers a clear explanation here. Five Vehmic judges in the Middle Ages condemned a man to death and executed the sentence themselves. In his previous life, this man had been a kind of chief and had ordered the death of the five. Then the chief had died and passed into kamaloca. During this period he was transported to the places where they now were, entering right into them, and experiencing what they had felt when they had been put to death. This is the starting-point of forces of attraction which bring human beings together when they return to the earth, in order that the law of karma may be fulfilled.

Such is the technique of karma, the way in which karma works. You see from this that there are forms of existence, kindred ties, which begin already on the astral plane. On the physical plane there is continuity of substance; on the astral plane, however, related yet separated parts of the bodily nature may be experienced. It is as if you were to feel your head, then nothing at all between head and heart, then the heart, then the feet, with nothing between heart and feet. One part of you may be in America, quite separated from but yet belonging to your astral being; another part may be on the moon and a third on yet another planet; there need be no visible astral connection between these parts of your being.

This view of the law of karma makes it clear that what arises in one human life-cycle is the outcome of many causes which lie in past lives. But how is the law of karma to be reconciled with heredity? It is said that there are many contradictions between heredity and this law.

People are apt to say of a morally sound person that he must be the offspring of a similarly sound family, that he must have inherited this from his forebears. When we observe the physical processes from the spiritual standpoint we know that it is not like this. We can, however, in a certain sense speak of processes of physical heredity, and we will take an example.

Within a period of 250 years, twenty-nine musicians were born in the Bach family, among them the great Bach himself.[16] A good musician needs not only the inner musical faculty but also a well-formed physical ear, a special form of ear. A lay person cannot perceive the differences here; it is necessary to look very deeply, with spiritual sight. Although the differences are very slight, a particular inner form of the organ of hearing is necessary if an individual is to become a musician, and these forms are transmitted by heredity; they resemble those that have been present in the parents, grandparents and so on.

Suppose that on the astral plane there is an individual who acquired great musical faculties hundreds or thousands of years ago; he is ready for reincarnation and is seeking a physical body. If he cannot find a physical body possessing suitable ears, he cannot become a musician. He must look around for a family that will provide the musical ear; without it his musical talents could not manifest, for the greatest virtuoso can do nothing without an appropriate instrument.

Mathematical talent also needs something quite specific. A particular construction of the brain is not, as many people think, necessary for mathematicians. Thinking, logic, is the same in the mathematician as in others. What is needed here is a special development of the three semi-circular canals in the ears, which lie in the three directions of space. Special development of these canals determines mathematical talent; herein lies the gift for mathematics. This is a physical organ and its form must be transmitted by heredity. You will remember that eight first-class mathematicians were born in the Bernoulli family.

A person of high moral principles also needs parents who

transmit a physical body suitable for the functioning of those moral gifts. So he has these parents and no others because he is this particular kind of individual.

The individuality seeks the parents, though under the guidance of higher beings. From the point of view of maternal love people take exception to this fact. They are fearful that they might lose something if the child were not to inherit certain qualities from the mother. True knowledge, however, shows maternal love to be something even more profound. It shows that this love is present before birth, even before conception, as a force which guided the child to the mother. The child loves the mother even before birth, and maternal love is the reciprocal force. Spiritually regarded, therefore, maternal love extends to the time before birth; it is rooted in mutual feelings of love.

It is often imagined that the human being is subject to an irrevocable law of karma in which nothing can be changed. Let us take a simile from everyday life to explain the working of this law.

A businessman enters debits and credits in his account books; taken together, these entries tell him the current state of his business. The financial state of his business is subject to the inexorable law governing the calculation of debit and credit. If he carries out any new transactions he can make additional entries and he would be a fool if he were unwilling to embark on further business once a balance had been drawn up. In respect of karma, everything good, intelligent and true that has been done by a person belongs on the credit side; evil or foolish deeds belong on the debit side. At every moment the individual is free to make new entries in the karmic book of life. It must never be imagined that life is under the sway of an immutable law of destiny; freedom is not impaired by the law of karma. In studying the law of karma, therefore, the future must be borne in mind as strongly as the past. Bearing within us the effects of past deeds, we are the slaves of the past, but the masters of the future. If we are to have a favourable future, we must make as many good entries as possible in the book of life.

It is a great and potent thought to know that nothing we do is in vain, that everything has its effect in the future. The law of karma is the reverse of depressing; it fills us with splendid hope, and knowledge of it is the most precious gift of spiritual science. It brings happiness inasmuch as it opens out a vista into the future. It charges us to be active for its sake; there is nothing whatever in it to make us sad, nothing which could give the world a pessimistic colouring; it lends wings to our will to co-operate in the evolution of the earth. Such are the feelings into which knowledge of the law of karma must be transmuted.

When a person is suffering, people sometimes say: 'He deserves his suffering and must bear his karma; if I help him, I am interfering with his karma.' This is nonsense. His poverty, his misery is caused through his earlier life, but if I help him, new entries will be made in his book of life; my help takes him forward. It would be foolish to say to a businessman who could be saved from disaster by 1,000 or 10,000 marks: 'No, for that would alter your balance-sheet.' It is precisely this possibility of altering the balance-sheet that should induce us to help someone. I help him because I know that nothing is without its karmic effect. This knowledge should spur us on to purposeful action.

Many people dispute the law of karma from the standpoint of Christianity, with theologians maintaining that Christianity cannot acknowledge this law because it is irreconcilable with the principle of Christ having died on the cross for the sake of all humanity. On the other hand there are theosophists who say that the law of karma contradicts the principle of the Redemption and that they cannot acknowledge the help given to the many by an individual. Both are wrong, for neither has understood the law of karma.

Suppose someone is in distress while you yourself are in a more fortunate position and can help him. By your help you make a new entry in his book of life. A more influential person can help two, and affect the karma of both of them. Someone still more powerful can help ten or a hundred people, and the most mighty of all can help unnumbered human beings. This does not in any way run counter to the principle of karmic connections. Precisely because of the absolute reliability of the law of karma we know that this help does indeed influence the destiny of the human being.

Humanity as a whole was very much in need of help when the Christ-Individuality was sent to the earth. The Redeemer's death on the cross, the death of one central Being, was the help that intervened in the karma of untold numbers of human beings. There is no variance between Christian esotericism and spiritual science when both are rightly understood. There is profound agreement between the laws of both and we are by no means obliged to abandon the principle of redemption.

We penetrate still more deeply into the law of karma when we study the evolution of humanity as a whole as well as the evolution of the earth. We have considered certain facts which help us to understand the law of karma, and we shall understand other facts still better when we pass on to the evolution of humanity itself, not only during the present earth period but also during the other planetary incarnations of the Earth. We shall discover certain supplementary details of this law when we go back to ages in the remote past, and receive indications, too, about the far future. By way of introduction we will consider a fact of great significance.

We have realized from what has been said that the external, physical body—the part of the human being that we see with physical eyes—is built up by the higher members of his being. Ego, astral body, ether body and all the members up to atma, the highest of them, work at the physical body. The various parts of our makeup, as they exist in us today, are not of equal but of different value in our nature. Even superficial consideration will make us realize that the physical body is the most perfect part of our nature. Take, for example, a part of the thigh-bone. This is not simply a compact, solid bone but a framework skilfully constructed out of intersecting beams. Anyone who studies this bone not only with the intellect but also with feeling will marvel at the wisdom which, in its creation, has used no more material than is essential to support the upper body with the smallest possible amount of strength. No engineering skill applied to the building of a bridge is equal to the wisdom that has brought such a bone into existence in nature.

If we investigate the human heart, but not merely with the eye of the anatomist or physiologist, we shall find in it an expression of sublime wisdom. Do not imagine that the human astral body today is as far advanced in development as the physical heart. The heart has been built up with skill and wisdom; the astral body with its desires induces the human being to consume all kinds of heart-poisons for many decades, yet the heart withstands this for many decades. Only in a future stage of evolution will the astral body have reached the stage of development of the physical body today, and then it will be at a far, far higher level than the physical body. Today the physical body is the most perfect; the ether body is less perfect, the astral body even less perfect, while the ego is the baby among the bodies.

The physical body as it is today is the oldest member of the human being; work has been performed on it for the longest period of time and not until it had reached a certain stage in the course of evolution did it become filled by the ether body.

After these two bodies had worked together for a time, the astral body was added, and finally, the 'I', the ego, which in the future will attain undreamed of heights of development. Just as the human being has repeated incarnations, so too has our earth passed through incarnations and will pass through still others in the future. Reincarnation is enacted throughout the cosmos. Our earth in its present form is the reincarnation of earlier planetary bodies of which there have been three. Before our earth became Earth, it was what is called by esotericism—not by astronomy—Moon. The present moon is in a way a body of dross which was discarded as useless.

If we could mingle the earth and the moon, together with all their substances and all their beings, we should have the 'occult Moon'—the forerunner of Earth. The earth of today is the remnant of Old Moon that remained after the dross had been thrown off. Just as the moon of today is a discarded remnant of the Old Moon incarnation of Earth, so is the sun in the heavens a body that proceeded from a still earlier incarnation of Earth. Before Earth was Moon it was, as we say in esotericism, Sun, and that Sun was composed of all the substances and beings which today form the sun, moon and earth. That Sun released itself from the substances and beings which form the earth and moon of today, which it could not, as a higher celestial body, retain, and it thereby became a fixed star. Spiritual researchers know that a fixed star need not always have been a fixed star; the sun only became a fixed star after having been a planet.

The sun we see today was once united with the earth and took with it many beings who were at a higher stage of development than the beings of the earth; just as the moon that we see took away the inferior portions, so that the moon is a body of discarded dross. The moon is a planet that has degenerated; the sun is a body that has ascended.

The Sun existence was preceded by the Saturn existence. Thus there are four consecutive incarnations of Earth: Saturn, Sun, Moon, Earth. When the forerunner of the human being was developing on Saturn, his only principle was that of the physical body; the ether body was added on Sun, the astral body on Moon, and the 'I' or ego on Earth.

The lecture entitled 'The Occult Significance of Blood' will have shown you how intimately the 'I' is connected with the blood.[17] This blood was not within the human body before the embodiment of an ego, so that this red human blood is connected with the evolution of Earth as such. It could not have been formed at all if Earth, in its evolutionary course, had not come together with another planet, namely with Mars. Before this contact of Earth with Mars, Earth had no iron; there was no iron in the blood; the blood upon which the human being is dependent today did not exist. In the first half of Earth evolution, the influence of the planet Mars is the ruling factor, while the influence of the planet Mercury rules in the second half.

Mars has given iron to the earth and the Mercury influence manifests on the earth in such a way that it makes the human soul more and more free, more and more independent. In esotericism, therefore, we speak of the Mars half of Earth evolution and of the Mercury half. Whereas the other names describe a whole planet, Earth evolution is spoken of as 'Mars-Mercury'. Used in this connection the names do not designate the planets we know today but the influences at work during the first and second halves of Earth evolution.

In the future, Earth will incarnate as a new planetary body, known as Jupiter. The human astral body then will have developed to a stage where it no longer confronts the physical body as an enemy, as is the case today, but it will still not have reached its highest stage. The ether body on Jupiter will have reached the stage at which the physical body is now, for it will then have three planetary evolutions behind it, as the physical body has today.

On the planetary body following Jupiter, the astral body will have developed as far as the physical body of today; it will have behind it the Moon, Earth and Jupiter evolutions and will have reached the Venus evolution. The final planetary incarnation will be that of Vulcan, when the 'I', the ego, will have attained the highest stage of its development. The future incarnations of Earth will thus be: Jupiter, Venus, Vulcan.

These designations are also found in the names of the days of the week. There was a time when the names of the things and facts around us in our lives were given by the initiates. People have no inner sense today of the way in which names really belong to things. The names given to the days of the week were meant to be reminders to human beings of their development through the evolutionary stages of Earth.

Saturday is Saturn-day; Sunday is Sun-day; Monday is Moon-day. Then Mars and Mercury, the two conditions of our earth: Tuesday is Mardi in French or Martedi in Italian; Wednesday is Mercredi in French or Mercoledi in Italian. Wotan is the same as Mercury: Tacitus spoke of Wotan's day, which is the English Wednesday. Then comes the Jupiter-day: in French it is Jeudi and in Italian Giovedi; Jupiter has affinities with Thor, hence Thursday in English. Venus-day is Vendredi in French and Venerdi in Italian; Venus is the Germanic Freyr, hence Friday in English, Freitag in German.

Thus in the names of the sequence of days in the week we have reminders of the development of Earth through its different incarnations.

# Human Consciousness in the Seven Planetary Incarnations

We will now consider the series of incarnations passed through by our planet, and realize that these were embodiments, that is to say, incarnations of the earth when it was once Saturn, then Sun and then Moon. We must be fully aware that these incarnations were necessary for the development of every living thing, especially the human being, and that human evolution itself is intimately connected with the evolution of Earth.

We shall, however, only understand in the right way what took place then if we realize how human beings of today—we ourselves—have changed in respect of certain characteristics in the course of evolution. First we will consider the changes that have come about in human consciousness. Everything in the world has evolved, even our consciousness. The consciousness we have today has not always existed; it has only gradually become what it is now.

We call our present consciousness the objective consciousness or the waking day-consciousness. You all know it as the consciousness you have from morning when you wake up until evening when you fall asleep. Let us be clear as to its character. It involves turning our senses towards the outer world and perceiving objects—and hence we call it objective consciousness.

We look around us and see with our eyes certain objects in space which are bounded by colours. We listen with our ears and perceive that there are objects in space that produce sounds. With our sense of touch we feel objects, find them warm or cold; we smell or taste objects. We then reflect upon what we thus perceive with our senses. We employ our reason to understand these different objects, and it is from these facts of sense perception and their comprehension in the mind that our present waking day-consciousness has arisen. Human beings have not always had this consciousness. It is something that had to develop; and they will not always have it as it is now, for it will ascend to higher stages.

With the means provided by spiritual science we can survey seven states of consciousness of which our present consciousness is the middle one; we can survey three preceding ones and three following after.

Many will wonder why we find ourselves placed so neatly in the centre. This comes from the fact that other stages, preceding the first, are beyond our sight, and that although yet others will follow the seventh, these again are beyond our sight. We can look backwards as far as forwards; if we were to retreat by one stage we should see one more behind and one fewer in front—just as when you go out into the fields you can see as far to the left as to the right.

These seven states of consciousness are the following. At first there was a very dull, deep state of consciousness which humanity hardly knows today. Only those with specific mediumistic capacities can still have this consciousness today which once upon Saturn was common to all human beings. Mediumistic individuals can enter such a consciousness, which is also known to modern psychologists. All the other states of consciousness became deadened in such people, and they appear to be virtually dead. But then, if from memory or even in this state they sketch or describe what they have experienced, they bring to light quite extraordinary experiences that do not take place around us. They make all sorts of drawings which, although they are grotesque and distorted, nevertheless agree with what in spiritual science we call cosmic conditions. They are often entirely incorrect, but nevertheless they have something by which we can recognize that such people during this lowered state have a dull but universal consciousness; they see cosmic bodies, and therefore they draw such things.

A consciousness that is dull like this but in compensation represents a universal knowledge of our cosmos, was once possessed by human beings on the first incarnation of Earth, and is called 'deep trance consciousness'. There are beings in our surroundings who still have such a consciousness—the minerals. If you could talk with them, they would tell you what goes on in Old Saturn—but this consciousness is entirely dull and insensible.

The second state of consciousness we know—or rather do not know, since we are then asleep—is that of ordinary sleep. This state is not so comprehensive, but in spite of still being very dull, it is clear in comparison with the first. This sleep-consciousness was once the permanent state of all human beings when the earth was Sun; at that time human ancestors were in a continuous sleep.

This state of consciousness still exists today; the plants have it. They are beings who uninterruptedly sleep, and if they could speak they would tell us how things were on Old Sun, for they have Sun-consciousness.

The third state, which is still dim and dull in relation to our day-consciousness, is that of picture-consciousness, and of this we have a clear idea since we experience an echo of it in our dream-filled sleep, though it is only a reminiscence of what on Moon was the consciousness of all human beings. It is a good idea to use dreams as a way of describing what Moon-consciousness was like.

There is something confusing, chaotic, about dream-life, but on closer observation this confusion nevertheless displays an inner law. The dream is a remarkable symbolist. In my lectures I have often given the following examples, which are all taken from life. You dream that you are running after a tree-frog to catch it, you feel the soft, smooth body; you wake up and have the corner of the sheet in your hand. Had you used your waking consciousness you would have seen how your hand was holding the bed-cover. Dream-consciousness gives you a symbol of the external act, it forms a symbol out of what our day-consciousness sees as a fact.

Another example: A student dreams that he is standing by the door in the lecture hall. There he is roughly jostled, and a challenge to a duel ensues. He now experiences every detail, until, accompanied by his second and a physician, he goes to the duel, and the first shot is fired. At this moment he wakes up, and sees that he has overturned the chair at his bedside. In waking consciousness he would simply have heard the fall; the dream symbolizes this prosaic event through the drama of the duel. You notice, also, that the timing is quite changed, for the whole drama flashed through his mind in the single instant during which the chair fell. The entire preparation for the duel took place in one moment; the dream has reversed time, it does not obey the circumstances of the ordinary world, it is a creator in time.

Not only can external events be symbolized in this way, but also inner processes of the body. Someone dreams he is in a dungeon; obnoxious spiders creep towards him. He wakes up and has a headache; his cranium has taken on the symbol of the dungeon, and the pain that of the hideous spiders.

Dreams dreamt by present-day human beings symbolize events that are both external and within. But it was not so when this third state of consciousness was that of Moon humanity. At that time human beings lived entirely in such pictures as they have in modern dreams, but then they expressed realities. They signified the same kind of reality as today the colour blue signifies a reality, only at that time colour hovered freely in space, it was not resting upon the objects. In that former consciousness people could not have set off down the street, as today, and then have seen a person in the distance, looked at him and approached him. The form of beings with a coloured surface could not have been perceived at that time, quite apart from the fact that human beings could not then walk as they do today.

When one human being on Moon met another, a freely hovering picture of form and colour would have risen up before him. If it had been ugly, he would have turned aside in order not to meet it; if beautiful, he would have gone towards it. The ugly colour-picture would have shown him that the other had an unsympathetic feeling towards him, the beautiful, that the other liked him.

Suppose there had been salt on Moon; when salt is on the table today, you see it as it is in space, as an object, granular, with definite colouring. At that time it would not have been so. On Moon you would not have been able to see the salt. But from the place where the salt was, a picture of colour and form would have proceeded, floating free; and this picture would have shown you that the salt was something useful.

Thus the whole of consciousness was filled with pictures, with floating colours and forms. The human being lived in an ocean of such form and colour pictures; and these pictures of colour and form denoted what was going on around him, above all, things of a soul character and those which affected the soul-nature—what was advantageous to him, or harmful. In this way the human being informed himself correctly about the things around him.

When Moon passed over into the Earth incarnation, this consciousness changed into our day-consciousness, and only a relic of it has remained in dreams as we now know them—a remnant, as there are remnants of other things also. You know, for instance, that there are certain muscles near the ear which nowadays seem purposeless. Formerly they had a purpose; they served to move the ears at will. Nowadays not many people can do this.

So conditions are to be found in the human being which have remained as a last relic of something that was once meaningful. Although such pictures no longer have a meaning, at that time they signified the outer world. Even today you still have this consciousness among those animals—note this carefully—which cannot utter sounds from their inner being. There is, in fact, a far truer categorization of animals in spiritual than in external science, namely into those that can utter sounds from within and those that are dumb. Of course some lower animals can produce sounds, but this happens mechanically, by friction and other means, and not from within. Even frogs do not utter sounds from within. Only the higher animals, those that arose at the time when human beings were able to express their suffering and joy with their voice, only these, together with human beings, have gained the power of expressing their pain and pleasure through vocal sounds and cries. All animals that do not utter sounds from within still have such a picture-consciousness. Lower animals do not see pictures in outlines as we do. If some lower animal, a crab, for example, perceives a picture that makes a distinctly unpleasant impression, it gets out of the way; it does not see the objects, but sees the harmfulness in a repelling picture.

The fourth state of consciousness is the one which all human beings now have. The pictures that earlier floated freely in space now wrap themselves, so to speak, round the objects. One might say they are laid over them, they form the surface and appear upon the objects, whereas formerly they seemed to float. In consequence, they have become the expression of the form; what human beings earlier had within themselves has come out and fastened itself on to the objects and through this we have come to our present waking day-consciousness.

We will now consider something else. We have already said that the human physical body was prepared on Saturn; on Sun the ether or life-body was added, which interpenetrated and worked on the physical. It took what the physical body had already become, and worked on it further. On Moon the astral body was added; this still further altered the form of the body. On Saturn the physical body was very simple, on Sun it was much more complicated, for then the ether body worked on it and made it more perfect. On Moon the astral body was added, and on Earth the ego, which brought it to a still greater completion. At the time when the physical body existed on Saturn, when as yet no ether body had interpenetrated it, it did not have all the organs it contains today, for it lacked blood and nerves, and also glands. The human being at that time merely had those organs—and these only in their rudiments—which today are the most perfect, and which have had time to arrive at their present perfection, namely the marvellously constructed sense organs.

The wonderful construction of the human eye, the wonderful apparatus of the human ear, all this has only attained its perfection today because it was formed out of the general substance of Saturn, and the ether body, astral body and ego have worked on it. So too the larynx; it was already incipient on Saturn, but human beings could not yet speak. On Moon they began to send out inarticulate sounds and cries, but only through the continuous activity described did the larynx become the perfected apparatus it is on our earth today. On Sun, where the ether body was added, the sense organs were further elaborated, and all those organs were added which are primarily organs of secretion and life, which serve the functions of nutrition and growth. They were incipient during the Sun stage of existence. Then the astral body worked further during Moon existence, the ego during Earth existence, and thus the glands, the organs of growth and so on have matured to their present perfection. Then on Moon the nervous system was the first to originate through the incorporation of the astral body. That was when human beings had picture-consciousness. The principle, however, which enabled them to evolve an objective consciousness and at the same time gave them the power to express pleasure and pain from within—the ego—this formed human blood.

The whole universe is the builder of the sense organs. All the glands, organs of reproduction and nutrition have been formed by the life-body, while the astral body has been the builder of the nervous system, and the ego the incorporator of the blood. There is a phenomenon termed anaemia or chlorosis in which the blood cannot sustain waking consciousness; sufferers often lapse into a dim consciousness like that on Moon.

Let us now consider the three states of consciousness that are still to come. One can ask how it is possible to know something about them already. It can be done through initiation. The initiate can have these states of consciousness even today, in anticipation. The next known to the initiate may be called the psychic consciousness,[18] a consciousness in which one has both together, picture-consciousness and waking day-consciousness. With this psychic consciousness you see a person in outline and form as in waking day-consciousness. But you see at the same time what lives in his soul, streaming out as coloured clouds and pictures into what we call the aura. Nor do you go about the world in a dreamy state like the Moon human being, but in complete self-control, as does a modern person of waking consciousness. On the planet that will replace Earth the whole of humanity will have this psychic or soul-consciousness, the Jupiter consciousness.

Then there is a sixth state of consciousness which human beings will one day possess. This will unite present day-consciousness, psychic consciousness now only known to the initiate, and in addition all that people today sleep through. Humans will look deeply into the nature of beings when they live in this consciousness, the consciousness of Inspiration. They will not only perceive in pictures and forms of colour, they will hear the being of the other giving forth sounds and notes. Each human individuality will have a certain note and the whole will sound together in a symphony. This will be the consciousness of human beings once our planet has passed into the Venus incarnation. There they will experience the harmony of the spheres which Goethe described in his Prologue to *Faust*:[19]

The sun makes music as of old
Amid the rival spheres of heaven,
On its predestined circle rolled
At thunder speed; ...

When Earth was Sun human beings were aware in a dim way of this ringing and resounding, and on Venus they will again hear it ringing and resounding 'as of old'. Down to this very phrase Goethe retained the picture.

The seventh state of consciousness is the spiritual consciousness,[20] the very highest, when the human being has a universal consciousness, when he will see not only what proceeds on his own planet, but in the whole cosmos round about. It is the consciousness that the human being had on Saturn, a kind of universal consciousness, although then quite dim and dull. This he will have in addition to all the other states of consciousness once he has reached Vulcan.

These are the seven states of human consciousness which the human being must go through on his journey through the cosmos. Each incarnation of Earth produces the conditions through which such states of consciousness are possible. Only because the system of nerves was laid down on Moon, and further developed to the present brain, has modern waking day-consciousness become possible. Organs must be created by which the higher states of consciousness may also have a physical basis of experience, as the initiate already experiences these states spiritually.

That the human being can pass through seven such planetary states of consciousness is the purpose of evolution. Each planetary stage is bound up with the development of one of the seven states of human consciousness, and through what takes place on each planet the physical organs for such a state of consciousness are perfected. You will have a more highly developed organ, a psychic organ, on Jupiter; on Venus there will be an organ through which the human being will be able to develop physically the consciousness possessed by the initiate today in the Devachanic plane. And on Vulcan the spiritual consciousness will prevail, which the initiate possesses today when he is in Higher Devachan, the world of reason.

Tomorrow we will examine these planets separately, for just as our earth, in the Atlantean and Lemurian ages for instance, once had a different appearance from that of today, and as later it will again look different, so too have Moon, Sun and Saturn passed through various conditions, and so will Jupiter and Venus pass through still others.

Today we have learnt the broad, comprehensive cycle of the planets; tomorrow we will occupy ourselves with the changes undergone by these planets while they were the theatre of human evolution.

Lecture 9

# Planetary Evolution I

We shall most easily understand the progress of humanity through the three incarnations that preceded Earth—Saturn, Sun, and Moon—if we first have another look at the sleeping, dreaming human being.

Observing someone who is asleep, the seer beholds the astral body with the ego enveloped in it as though floating above the physical body. The astral body is outside the physical and ether bodies, but remains connected with them. It sends threads—or rather currents—into the universal body of the cosmos, and seems as though embedded in it. Thus in the sleeping person we have the physical, the etheric and the astral bodies, with the latter sending out feelers towards the great astral universe.

If we picture this condition as an enduring one, if here on the physical plane there were only human beings who had the physical body interpenetrated with the etheric body, while above hovered over them an astral soul with the ego, then we should have the condition in which humanity existed on Moon, except that on Moon the astral body was not strongly separated from the physical body; it immersed itself in the physical body to the same degree as it expanded into the cosmos.

Now picture a state of sleep where no dream ever comes. This shows you the condition in which humanity existed on Sun. Then go on to imagine a human being who has died, so that even his ether body is outside the physical and united to the astral body and ego, although the link is still not quite severed. Imagine that what is outside, embedded in the whole surrounding cosmos, is sending down its rays and working upon the physical substance; this shows you the condition in which humanity existed on Saturn.

Down there on the cosmic globe of Saturn there was only what we have in our purely physical body; it was surrounded, so to speak, by an etheric-astral atmosphere, in which the egos were embedded.

Human beings were already in existence on Saturn but in an extremely dulled state of consciousness. These souls had the task of maintaining in an active and mobile state something that belonged to them down there below. They worked from above on their physical body, like a snail fashioning its shell; they acted from outside, like a tool, on the bodily organs. We will describe the appearance of what the souls worked on from above; we must give some little description of this physical Saturn as such.

I have already said that the part of the physical body elaborated there was the foundation of the sense organs. The souls worked from without upon the Saturn surface, upon what lived in human beings as rudiments of the senses. They were in the cosmic space surrounding Saturn, and down below were their workshops where they worked out the archetypes for eyes and ears and the other sense organs.

What was the fundamental quality of this Saturn-substance? It is hard to characterize, for we have scarcely a word in our language which is suitable; our words are quite materialized and are only adapted to the physical plane. There is one word, however, which can express the delicate work that was being carried out there. The verb 'to reflect' describes it. The Saturn globe in all its parts had the capacity to reflect everything—such as light, sound, fragrance, taste—that reached it from outside; all this was reflected back again; in cosmic space one perceived these things as reflections in the mirror of Saturn. One can only compare it with the effect of looking into the eye of another human being, and seeing our own image in miniature looking out from it towards us.

In this way all human souls were aware of themselves, but not only as a picture in colour; they perceived themselves in taste, in fragrance, in a specific feeling of warmth. Saturn was thus a reflecting planet. The human beings living in the atmosphere cast their essence and being into it, and out of the pictures that then arose, the rudiments of the sense organs began to take shape, for they were pictures that worked creatively. Imagine yourself in front of a mirror from which your own image confronts you, and that this image begins to create, that it is not a dead image as in our modern lifeless mirror. There you have the creative activity of Saturn, there you have the kind of way human beings lived on Saturn and accomplished their work.

This took place down below on the Saturn globe; up above, the souls were in the deep trance consciousness of which I spoke yesterday. They knew nothing of this mirroring, yet they brought it about. In this dull trance consciousness they had within them the entire cosmic All, and thus the whole cosmic All was mirrored from their being. They themselves, however, were embedded in a basic substance of a spiritual kind. They were not independent but were only one part of the spirituality surrounding Saturn. They could not therefore have a spiritual perception; higher spirits perceived by means of them. They were the organs of perception for other spirits.

A whole number of higher spirits lived in the surroundings of Saturn; all those whom Christian esotericism called the divine messengers, angels, archangels, primal forces, powers of revelation. All these were contained in the Saturn atmosphere. Just as the hand belongs to the organism as a whole, so did the souls belong to these beings; and just as little as the hand has an independent consciousness, so little had they at that time a consciousness of their own. They worked out of the consciousness of higher beings, the consciousness of a higher world; they thus fashioned the forms of their sense organs, which then became creative, and they also moulded the Saturn substance. You must not think of this substance of Saturn as being as dense as human flesh is today. The very densest condition that it could attain was not even as dense as our present physical air. Saturn did become physical, but it only reached the density of fire, of heat or warmth in which our modern physics no longer discerns any physical material at all. For the spiritual scientist, however, heat is a finer substance than gas; it has the characteristic of continuous expansion. And since Saturn consisted of this substance it had the power of spreading from within outwards, of raying out everything, of reflecting. Such a body radiates everything; it has no need to keep it all within itself.

Saturn was not a uniform substance but of such a composition that one could have perceived a differentiation, a configuration. Later the organs became rounded into cell-shaped balls, except that while cells are small these were larger, resembling a mulberry or blackberry. You could not as yet have had sight on Saturn, for the reflecting process threw all light that came from outside back again. Within this Saturn substance all was dark; only towards the end of its evolution did it begin to light up a little. A number of beings were present in the surrounding atmosphere of Saturn. You yourselves were not alone in working on your sense organs, for the human soul was not yet so far developed as to be able to work alone. You worked in conjunction with other spiritual beings, under their guidance so to speak.

Certain beings worked on Saturn as independently as modern human beings today; they were then at the human level. They could not have the shape of modern human beings, for heat was the only substance of Saturn. In respect of their intelligence, their ego-consciousness, however, they were at the level of present human beings, though they could form no physical body, no brain. Let us observe them more closely. The present-day human being consists of four members: physical body, ether body, astral body and ego; and prefigured in the ego are spirit-self, life-spirit and spirit-man (manas, buddhi, atma). The lowest, although of its kind the most perfect member on the Earth planet, is the physical body. The next higher is the ether body, then the astral body and the ego. There are also beings who have no physical body, whose lowest member is the ether body. They have no need of the physical body in order to be active in our sense-world; in compensation they have a member that is higher than our seventh.

Others have the astral body as their lowest member and in compensation a ninth; and again others, who have the ego as their lowest member, have in compensation a tenth member. When we consider the beings who have the ego as lowest member we have to say they consist of: ego, spirit-self, life-spirit, spirit-man. Then come the eighth, ninth and tenth members, which are what Christian esotericism calls the Holy Trinity: Holy Spirit, Son or Word, Father. In theosophical literature one is accustomed to call these the three Logoi.

These beings, whose lowest member is the ego, are those who come into special consideration for us in the Saturn evolution. They were at the stage which humanity has reached today. They were able to exercise their ego under those quite different conditions that I have described. They were the human beings of Saturn, and the predecessors of our present humanity. They irradiated the surface of Saturn with their egohood, their most external nature. They were the implanters of egohood in the physical corporeality that was forming on the surface of Saturn.

Thus they made it their care to prepare the physical body in such a way that it could later become the bearer of the ego.

Only such a physical body as you have today, with feet, hands and head and the sense organs incorporated in it, could be the ego-bearer at the fourth stage, Earth. For this to come about the seed had to be implanted on Saturn. One also calls these ego-beings of Saturn: Spirits of Egoism.[21]

Egoism has two sides, one admirable, the other objectionable. If at that time on Saturn and on the succeeding planets the essential nature of egoism had not again and again been implanted, the human being would never have become an independent being who can say 'I' to himself. Into your bodily nature there has been instilled ever since Saturn the sum of forces which stamps you as an independent being, separating you off from all other beings. To this end the Spirits of Egoism, the Asuras, had to work.

There are two kinds of these, apart from a few slight degrees of difference. The one kind has elaborated egoism in a noble, self-reliant way that has risen higher and higher in the perfection of the sense of freedom: this is the admirable independence of egoism. These spirits have guided humanity through all the successive planets; they have become the educators of humanity towards independence.

At every planetary stage there are also spirits who have remained behind in evolution, they have remained stationary and not wished to progress. You will recognize a law from this: if the most admirable falls and commits the 'great sin' of not advancing with evolution, then it becomes the very worst of all. The noble sense of freedom has been reversed into something objectionable, its opposite. These are the Spirits of Temptation, and we must pay grave attention to them; they lead to the objectionable side of egoism. Even today they are still all around us, these evil spirits of Saturn. All that is bad draws its power from these spirits.

When each planet has completed its evolution it becomes spiritual again. It is, so to speak, no longer in existence; it passes over into a state of sleep in order later to come forth once more. Thus it was with Saturn. Its next incarnation is Sun, a Sun which you would obtain if you were to mix together as in a cauldron all that is on the sun, the moon and the earth, together with all the terrestrial and spiritual beings. Sun evolution is distinguished by the fact that the ether body entered into the physical body prepared down below. Sun had a denser substantiality than Saturn; it can be compared with the density of our present air. The human physical substance, your own body which you formed for yourselves, is to be seen on Sun interpenetrated by the ether body. You yourselves belonged to a body of air, as on Saturn to a body of heat. Your ether body was already down below, while your astral body with your ego remained enveloped in the great general astral body of Sun. There you worked down into the physical and ether bodies, just as you do in sleep today when your astral body is outside and works upon the physical and ether bodies. At that time you were elaborating the first rudiments of all that today are organs of growth, digestion and reproduction. You were transforming the elementary sense organs of Saturn, some of which maintained their character, while others were transformed into glands and organs of growth. All organs of growth and organs of reproduction are sense organs taken hold of by the ether body and transformed.

When you compare the body of Sun with Saturn you find a specific difference. Saturn was still like a reflecting surface; it rayed back everything it received in the way of taste, smell and all sense-perceptions. This was not so on Sun. Whereas Saturn rayed back everything direct, without taking possession of it, Sun first absorbed it and then rayed it back, being able to do so by virtue of having an ether body. Its body, penetrated by an ether body, did as the plant does today with sunlight. The plant takes up the sunlight, absorbs it and then gives it back again. If it is put in some dark place, it loses its colour and wilts. There would be no green colouring without light. So it was with your own body on Sun; it absorbed light and also other ingredients, and as the plant sends back the light after having drawn strength from it, so did Sun once upon a time ray back the light after having worked it over inwardly. It filled itself not only with the light, but also with taste, fragrance, heat, everything, and radiated it all out again.

Hence on Sun your own body, too, was at the stage of the plant. It did not look like a plant in the modern sense, for this has only been formed on Earth. What you bear within you in the way of glands, organs of growth and reproduction were upon Sun as mountains and rocks are on the earth today. You worked on them as you nowadays tend and cultivate a little garden. Sun radiated back the ingredients of cosmic space; it shone in the loveliest colours. A wonderful sound rang forth, an exquisite aroma streamed out. Old Sun was a wonderful being in cosmic space. Thus at that time on Sun human beings worked at their own bodily substance like certain creatures, corals for instance, work from outside on their structure. This took place under the guidance of higher beings, for there were higher beings in Sun's atmosphere.

We must concern ourselves with one special category of these who had at that time achieved the level reached by human beings today. On Saturn we have the Spirits of Egoism who implanted the sense of freedom and self-reliance and had attained the human level. On Sun it was other beings who had as their lowest member not the ego but the astral body. They possessed astral body, ego, spirit-self, life-spirit and spirit-man, and the eighth member, named the Holy Spirit in Christian esotericism, and finally the ninth member, the Son, the 'Word' in the sense of the Gospel of John. As yet they did not have the tenth member, but instead, as their lowest, the astral body. These were the spirits who were active on Sun, they guided all the astral activity. They differ from modern human beings inasmuch as human beings breathe air, since air is in the earthly environment; these spirits, however, breathed heat or fire.

Sun was itself a kind of being of air, surrounded by that substance which had previously formed Saturn: fire, heat. The part that had densified had formed the gaseous Sun, and what had not densified was a surging sea of fire. These beings were able to live on Sun and inhale and exhale heat, fire; they are therefore called the Spirits of Fire. They were at the human level on Sun and they worked in the service of humanity. One calls them Sun Spirits or Fire Spirits. Human beings at that time were at the stage of sleep-consciousness, whereas the Sun-Fire Spirits had already attained ego consciousness. Since then they have developed further and ascended to higher degrees of consciousness. In Christian esotericism they are called archangels. The highest evolved Spirit who was on Sun as a Fire Spirit, who today is still active upon the earth, with very highly-evolved consciousness, this Sun or Fire Spirit is the Christ. In the same way the most evolved Saturn Spirit is the Father God.

Christian esotericism knows that incarnated in the body of flesh and blood of Christ Jesus there was precisely such a Sun-Fire Spirit, indeed, the highest, the Ruler of the Sun Spirits. To come to the earth he had to make use of a physical body; he had to live under the same earthly conditions as human beings in order to be able to be active here.

On Sun, then, we are concerned with a Sun-body, as it were, a body of the Sun planet with Ego-Spirits, who are Fire Spirits, and with a Ruler of the Sun, the most highly evolved, the Christ. When Earth was Sun, this Spirit was the central Spirit of the Sun; when Earth was Moon, he was more highly developed, but he remained with Moon; when Earth was the earth, he was most highly developed and remained with the earth having united himself with it after the Mystery of Golgotha. Thus he is the highest planetary Spirit of Earth. Earth today is his Body as previously Sun was his Body. Therefore you must take literally the words of the John Gospel: Whoever eats my bread, treads me underfoot.[22] For the earth is the Body of Christ. When human beings, who eat the bread taken from the body of the earth, walk upon the earth, they tread underfoot the Body of Christ. Take these words quite literally, as all religious documents must be taken, only one must first know the true meaning of the letters and then seek for the spirit.

Now something else. Not all beings within this Sun-mass came to the stage of evolution of which I have spoken. Many stayed behind at the stage of Saturn existence. They were unable to receive into themselves what streamed in from cosmic space and send it back after receiving it; they had to send it back direct, without first absorbing it. These beings therefore appeared on Sun like some kind of dark encapsulations that could not send out their own light. Since they were enclosed in the Sun-mass surrounded by a mass sending out its own light, they appeared like dark patches. We must therefore distinguish between those places on Sun which radiated out into cosmic space what they had received, and those which could not radiate anything. Thus they appeared as dark insertions within the Sun-mass; they had learnt nothing new on Saturn. Just as in the human body you do not find glands and organs of growth everywhere, but the body is interspersed with dead parts which have been incorporated, so was Sun interspersed with these dark insertions.

Our present sun is the descendant of the Earth-Sun-body. It has cast out the moon and the earth and has retained the most advanced part. What was present in the former Sun-body as relics of Saturn are still to be found in the present sun, in what we call the sun-spots. They are the last vestiges of Saturn, which remain in the shining sun-mass as dark insertions. Our esoteric wisdom discloses the hidden spiritual sources of physical facts. Physical science substantiates the physical causes of the sun-spots through its astronomy and astro-physics; the spiritual causes, however, lie in that residue remaining from Saturn.

We now ask what kingdoms were there on Saturn? Only one, the last traces of which are contained in the present mineral kingdom. When we speak of the human being passing through the mineral kingdom, we must not think of present-day minerals. The last descendants of Saturn mineral must rather be seen in your eyes, ears and other sense organs. These are the most physical, the most mineral parts of you. The apparatus of the eyes is like a physical instrument and even continues unchanged for some time after death.

The single Saturn kingdom progressed on Sun to become a kind of plant existence. There we encounter the human body growing like a plant. What was left behind as Saturn kingdom became a kind of mineral kingdom on Sun, which had the form of stunted sense-organs that could not reach their goal. But all these beings on Sun which were developing human bodies had as yet no nervous system within them. That was incorporated for the first time on Moon by the astral body. Plants, too, have no nervous system and therefore no sentient capacity. It is an error to ascribe sentience to them.

But the astral bodies, especially those that proceeded from the Fire Spirits, sent a kind of stream into the substance that was down below as physical and etheric bodies. These streams of light divided in tree-like forms. Their last traces are to be found in densified, external form as the organ we call the solar plexus. This goes back to the ancient instreaming on Sun, densified to substance, and hence the term *solar* plexus.

You must picture the bodies which you had on Sun as if currents from above streamed into you, currents interlaced as a branching tree. Thus Sun is represented in the numberless interlacings which are your solar plexus. In Germanic mythology these branchings were represented as the World Ash-tree which, however, signifies very much else besides.

Then Sun passed into a state of sleep and was transformed into what in spiritual science we call Moon. This was a third incarnation of Earth, which will again introduce to us a directing central Spirit. The highest Ruler of Saturn, the Ego Spirit, appears to us as the Father God, and the highest Ruler of Sun, the Sun-God, as the Christ. Similarly the Ruler of the Moon stage of Earth appears to us as the Holy Spirit with his hosts known in Christian esotericism as the Messengers of the Godhead, the angels.

We have now accomplished our study of two days of creation, which in esoteric language are called *Dies Saturni* and *Dies Solis*. To them we must add *Dies Lunae*, the Moon day. The existence of a directing Godhead of Saturn, Sun and Moon has always been known.

The words *dies* (day) and *deus* (god) have the same origin, so that *dies* may be translated either as Day or Godhead. So for *Dies Solis* one can equally well say Sun-Day or Sun-God, meaning the Christ Spirit in both cases.

# Lecture 10

# Planetary Evolution II

We spoke yesterday about the various incarnations of our planet, about the Saturn and Sun incarnations, and we will only briefly bring to mind that the human being on the Sun-planet, the forerunner of our Earth, was developed to the degree of having a physical and an ether body, and that he had therefore risen to a kind of plant-existence. I also told you how different this plant existence was from what you know as the plant world in your environment today. We shall see that plants as they surround us today have only arisen on our planet earth. We also described to a certain extent how these human forerunners on Sun, inasmuch as they had an ether body, brought to expression in the physical body chiefly those organs that we know nowadays as the glandular organs of growth, reproduction and nutrition. All this was to be seen on Sun just as on the earth we now see rocks, stones and plants. There was in addition a kingdom that we can call a retarded Saturn kingdom, which contained the elements of the later minerals. There is no question of minerals as we know them today being present on Sun, but there were bodies that had not acquired the power of receiving an ether body and which had therefore in a certain respect remained behind at the mineral stage through which human beings had formerly passed on Saturn.

We must therefore speak of two kingdoms having been formed on Sun. In theosophical writings people have become accustomed to say that human beings have gone through the mineral, the plant and the animal kingdoms. You have seen that this is an inexact way of talking, since the mineral kingdom on Saturn was quite differently formed. In its formations the first seeds, the earliest indications of our sense organs were prefigured. Nor was there a plant kingdom on Sun like the present one, but all that lives in human beings today as organs of growth was of a plant-like nature, i.e. all glandular organs. They were plant-like because they were permeated by an ether body.

We must now imagine that this Sun-existence passed through a kind of sleep condition, a darkening, a dormant period. You must not think, however, that the passing of a planet through a state of sleep meant a sort of inactivity, a condition of nothingness. It is as little inactive as the Deva-chan condition of the human being. The human Devachanic state is not an inactive one; on the contrary, we have seen that human beings exist there in continuous activity, and co-operate in the development of Earth in the most important way, only for the modern consciousness of human beings it is a kind of sleep state. To a different consciousness, however, it appears as a much more active, more real condition. All these transition periods denote a passing through celestial, higher conditions in which important things are carried out for the planetary incarnations. The theosophical expression for them is 'Pralaya'.

We will now imagine that Sun has passed through such a condition and that from Sun there has developed the third stage of our Earth, called Moon in esotericism. If we had been able to observe this process, we should have been shown something like the following: we should have seen in the course of millions of years how the Sun existence changed and disappeared, and after further millions of years how it lit up again after a twilight state. This is the beginning of the Moon cycle.

When Sun first lit up again there was no question of a division between the sun and the moon; they were still together as in the Sun period. Then came what one calls a recapitulation of the earlier conditions; what had taken place on Saturn and Sun was recapitulated at a certain higher stage. Then a remarkable alteration took place in the condition of this newly emerged Sun. Moon gathered itself into a mass apart from Sun; two planets, or rather a fixed star and a planet arose from the old Sun system, a larger and a smaller body were formed: the sun and moon. The Moon stage I now mean contained not only what the present moon contains, but rather all the various substances and beings contained in the present earth and moon. If you were to stir all this together you would have that Moon of which we are speaking and which at that time had separated itself off from the sun.

Sun became a fixed star by reason of drawing out the best substances together with the spiritual beings. As long as it was a planetary Sun existence it still contained all of this within itself. But since it now gave up to an independent planet everything that had hindered the beings in their higher development it became a fixed star. So now we have the cosmic scene before us of a more highly evolved body as fixed star, and moving round this in space a planet that is of lesser worth—Moon—containing within it what is today both the moon and the earth.

This movement of Moon round Sun was quite different from the movement of our present earth. If you examine the latter you can distinguish two movements. First, the earth travels round the sun, and secondly it revolves round its own axis. Through the latter movement, which takes place approximately 365 times in a year, day and night arise, as you know, and through the former the four seasons. This, however, was not the case with Old Moon. That Moon was, you could say, a more polite body to its Sun than our earth is, for it always moved round the Sun in such a way as to show it the same side; it never turned its back on it. While it passed once round the Sun it turned only once round itself. Such a different kind of movement, however, had a great effect on the beings who were evolving on that planet.

I will now describe to you the Moon planet itself. Here I must add, first of all, that the human being was again a little more advanced than on Sun or Saturn. He had come so far as to consist not only of physical body and ether body, but there was now the astral body in addition. We therefore now have a human being formed of physical body, ether body and astral body, but as yet no ego. The consequence was that Moon human beings progressed to the third state of consciousness we have described, picture consciousness, the last relic of which we have in the dream-picture consciousness of today. By virtue of the incorporation of the astral body into the other bodies, changes took place in these, and especially in the physical body. We have seen that on Sun the glandular organs were the most highly developed part of the physical body, and that certain places were interpenetrated by currents which later hardened to the present solar plexus. Through the work of the astral body upon the physical body on Moon arose the first beginnings of the nervous system; the nerves attached themselves in a way similar to what you still have today in the nerves of the spinal cord.

Consider one thing. Human beings had as yet no independent ego; only the three other bodies were there. The human ego was in the atmosphere surrounding Moon, just as formerly the ether body had been on Saturn and the astral body on Sun, and from there this ego, embedded in its divine source, worked upon the physical body. If we remember that at that time the ego still worked as a companion of divine beings, that it had not yet emancipated itself, had not yet fallen out of this divine spiritual essentiality, then we see that the ego in its path to earth has undergone in a certain way a kind of deterioration and in another way also an advance; an advance inasmuch as the ego has become independent, a deterioration, however, in that it has now become exposed to all doubt, errors, wickedness and evil.

The egos worked from the divine-spiritual substance. An ego that today works down from the astral plane on to the physical plane is a group-soul of the animals. The ego at that time worked into the three bodies from outside in the way these group-souls today work into the animals. It could, however, create higher bodies than those of the present animal kingdom since it worked from the divine substance. There were living creatures on Moon which in appearance and in their whole nature were higher than the highest apes today, but not so high as present human beings. There was an intermediate kingdom between present human beings and the animal kingdom. Then there were two more kingdoms, both of which had become retarded. One of these had not been capable of taking up the astral body after the Sun existence and had therefore remained at the stage in which the gland-ular organs were on Sun. This second kingdom of Moon lay between the present animals and the present plants; it was a kind of plant-animal. On earth today there is no directly similar creature; we can only recognize relics of it. There was also a third kingdom, which had preserved the Saturn incar-nation even on Sun; it came between mineral and plant. Thus on Moon we have three kingdoms: plant-mineral, animal-plant, and human-animal.

The minerals of today on which we walk about did not exist on Moon; what we call rocks, soil, humus did not exist there. The lowest kingdom came between plant and mineral. The whole substance of Moon consisted of this kingdom. The surface of Moon somewhat resembled peat in which plants are in the process of turning into a kind of pulpy mass. Moon beings went about on a vegetable-mineral mass of pulp-like consistency. This was the state on Moon during certain periods of its development—one might also compare it with boiled lettuce.\* There were no rocks in the present sense, the nearest thing to them being certain formations occurring here and there which you can compare with the growths formed by the wood or bark of certain trees. The Moon-mountains consisted of such lignification, such wood masses of lignified plant pulp. It was like a kind of aged plant that has withered. This was the earliest beginning of the mineral kingdom and upon it flourished those plant-animals; they could make no independent movements, they were fixed to the ground, as corals are today.

In our myths and legends, which contain deep wisdom given by initiates, a memory is preserved of this, above all in the legend of the death of Balder. The Germanic sun-god or god of light once had a dream in which his approaching death was foretold. This made the gods, the Aesir, who loved him, very sad; they wondered how they might save him. The mother of the gods, Frigg, put all the beings of the earth on solemn oath that not one of them would ever kill Balder. They all swore and so it seemed impossible that Balder should ever fall victim to death. Then one day the gods were at play, and during their game they threw every possible sort of thing at Balder without hurting him; they knew that he was invulnerable. Loki, however, the god of darkness and the opponent of the Aesir, mused on how to kill Balder. Then he heard from Frigg that she had made all beings swear not to kill him. Far away, however, there was a plant, the mistletoe, which was harmless and she had administered no oath to it; this she disclosed to him. The crafty Loki took the mistletoe and brought it to the blind god, Hodur, and he, not knowing what he did, killed Balder with it. So the evil dream was fulfilled through the mistletoe. It has always played a special role in

---

\* '*Kochsalat*' (Tr.)

popular custom; something sinister, ghostly, was expressed through it. What was taught about the mistletoe in the old Trotten and Druid Mysteries passed over to the populace as legend and custom.

These are the facts: on Moon there was that mineral-plant pulp and upon it flourished the plant-animals of Moon. There were some that evolved further and reached a higher stage on Earth; others, however, had stayed behind at the Moon stage, and as Earth arose could only assume a stunted form; they had to continue with the habits they had had on Moon. On the earth they could only live as spongers, parasites on a plant-like foundation. So the mistletoe lives on other trees since it is a relic of the old plant-animals of Moon.

Balder was the expression of what evolves further, of what brings light to Earth; Loki, on the contrary, the representative of the dark powers, the backward powers, hates what has progressed and has gone on developing. Therefore Loki is the opponent of Balder. None of the creatures of Earth could undertake anything against Balder, the god who gave light to Earth, for they were his equals, they had progressed with evolution. Only a being still at the Moon stage and feeling itself united with the ancient god of darkness was capable of killing the god of light. Mistletoe is also a remedy, as are many poisons. Thus do we find deep facts of cosmic wisdom in old folklore and customs.

Let us now call to mind the beings on Saturn who had the ego as the outermost body, and remember that on Sun there were such as had the astral body as their external covering. On Moon there were beings whose external covering was the ether body. They consisted of ether body, astral body, ego, spirit-self, life-spirit and spirit-man, and of one member more, the eighth,[23] the Holy Spirit, of which we cannot yet speak in the case of human beings today. We could only have seen them as phantom-like beings in their ether body; they had at that time the same degree of evolution as human beings today. Christian esotericism calls them angels. They are beings who today are placed directly above the human being since they have evolved to the stage of the Holy Spirit. They are also called Spirits of Twilight or the Lunar Pitris.[24]

The Spirits of Egohood on Saturn had as their leader a Being whom human beings call the Father-God. The Spirits of Fire on Sun had as their leader the Christ or, in the sense of the John Gospel, the Logos. On Moon the leader was the Spirit known in Christianity as the Holy Spirit. Those beings who had passed through the human stage on Moon had no need to descend as far as the physical body here on the earth.

The planetary formations have become ever denser and denser. Old Saturn in its densest state had only a heat consistency. Sun in its densest state consisted of what we see today in gases, in air, although you must picture these substances as somewhat denser than our present heat-substance and gases. In the Moon stage the gaseous substances of Sun had so far densified that they produced that pulpy, thickish, fluid, flowing mass of which all the beings, even the highest, the animal-humans, consisted on Moon. You have more or less this substance if you imagine the white of a hen's egg somewhat thickened. Into this substance of the human being the nervous system was incorporated.

Moon was surrounded by a kind of atmosphere formed quite differently from that of the earth. We understand its character if we think of a passage in Goethe's *Faust*; it is where Mephistopheles wants to rise into the air with Faust on his cloak, he wants to make fire-air—air in which watery substances are dissolved mist-like.[25] This air saturated with watery substances—it is also called fire-air or fire-mist—was breathed by the beings of Moon. They had no lungs; even the highest beings breathed through something akin to gills, as present-day fishes do.

This fire-air, called 'ruach' in the Hebrew tradition, can actually be made manifest in a particular way. 'Ruach' has been lost to modern man, but the old alchemists were able to set up the necessary conditions for it, and could bring elemental beings into their service by means of it. This fire-mist was thus something fully understood in old alchemical times, and the further back we go, the more capable people were of producing it. The atmosphere our predecessors breathed on Moon was fire-mist like this. It has continued to evolve and has differentiated itself into our present air and into whatever has arisen on the earth under the influence of fire.

The smoke-like, steam-like Moon atmosphere, which had a certain temperature, was interpenetrated, sometimes more, sometimes less, by currents which hung down from the air rather like threads, and sank into the human bodies and permeated them. The human body on Moon hung on a kind of strand which extended into the atmosphere, as today the child in the womb hangs on the umbilical cord. It was like a cosmic umbilical cord, and out of the fire-mist certain substances entered the bodies comparable to what human beings create today, their blood. The 'I' or ego was outside the human being and sent through these cords into the bodies something similar to blood, and this substance streamed in and out of them. The beings never came in contact with the Moon surface; they hovered and circled around it, as if they were flowing and floating. The Moon human-animals moved as today's aquatic animals move in water. It was the work of the angels, the Spirits of Twilight, to let these blood-juices flow into human beings.

Those very different conditions had another consequence. On Moon a kind of blood-system began. From the cosmos a substance resembling blood streamed in and out, as now the air streams in and out of the body, and therefore there arose for Moon human beings a capacity which only appears with the blood. This was the first sounding of inner notes for expressing experiences of the soul. It is only when beings possess an astral body that sentience arises, and they could express this sentience in sounds, and indeed in a remarkable way. They were not clearly formed sounds, they could not have cried out with pain; there was no independence of giving vent to sound, of crying out, but it occurred simultaneously with certain experiences. At definite seasons there took place on Moon what one could call a development of the reproductive impulses, and the inner experiences of the beings at those times could be expressed in sound; otherwise they were silent. At a definite position of Moon to the sun, in a certain season, Old Moon sounded forth into the cosmos. The beings upon it cried out their germinative power into the cosmos. We have relics of this preserved in the cries of some animals, the stag, for example. The cry was more the precipitation of general processes, not of individual experiences which are voluntarily expressed. A cosmic event was finding its expression.

We must take all this as only an approximate description, for we are bound to words which are coined for things that have only come into existence in our Earth period. We should first have to invent a language if we wanted to express what is seen by the eye of the seer. All the same, these descriptions are important, for they are the first approach to finding a way of expressing the truth. Only through pictures, through Imagination, do we find the way to vision. We should make no abstract concepts, no mechanical schemes, nor draw up diagrams of vibrations, but let pictures arise within us; that is the direct path, the first stage of knowledge. For as surely as human beings were present at that time with their forces, so is it true that if they picture things to themselves, this will guide them to the conditions in which they then existed.

After all the beings on Moon had passed through their

evolution and could ascend to higher stages, the time came when Moon and the sun again united, reverted to being a single body and so entered into Pralaya. After they had gone through this dormant stage together, a new existence shone out, the earliest proclamation of Earth as such.

A short recapitulation of the first three incarnations now took place on a higher level. First Saturn existence, then Sun; and then Moon once more split off and circled round the other body. But this Moon still had Earth within it.

Then came a further highly important change. All that is Earth threw out of itself the present moon, which means the worst substances and beings, whatever is unserviceable, and these are contained in the present moon. All that was flowing watery substance in Old Moon, is frozen on the present moon (this can be proved by physical means); and what was capable of developing further remained behind as Earth. Higher development continues on Earth through the separation of Old Sun into these three bodies: sun, moon and earth.

This separation happened many thousands of years ago, in the old Lemurian time.[26] From those ancient Moon-beings, which have been described as plant-mineral, plant-animal and animal-human have arisen the present mineral, the present plant, the present animal and the human being who has become able to receive into himself the ego which formerly hovered around him and was united with the Godhead. The union of the 'I' or ego with the human being took place after the separation of sun, moon and earth, and from this point of time onwards the human being has been capable of developing red blood within himself, and of ascending to the level he has reached today.

# The Evolution of Humanity on the Earth I

We have come in our studies to the point where Earth has passed through what we termed the Moon stage. We have also seen that a kind of sleep-state of the whole system followed the Moon stage of Earth. One must of course realize that all the beings who inhabit the planet share these transitional, inter-mediate states with it. During this time they pass through experiences differing from those of the external state of evo-lution. We will try to be clear as to how the beings have undergone various things in the transition between the Moon stage of Earth and the actual Earth evolution.

We saw that three kinds of being lived on Moon, physical forebears, so to say, of our present nature kingdoms. There existed a kind of plant-mineral, animal-plant and human-animal. Human beings as such on this Old Moon had not yet developed ego-consciousness. So far human beings had not attained to an 'I', an ego, dwelling within a body.

During this transitional period something very important came about in the spiritual part of the human being—if I may use this term.

If we form a true picture of the Old Moon sphere, we could describe it as a being which itself possessed a sort of life, somewhat like a tree, upon which all manner of living things exist. Moon itself was a kind of homogeneous plant-mineral. Its rocks were only a hardening of the plant-mineral mass, and its animal-plants grew out of the mass, while what we can call the human-animals circled around Moon. We must at the same time be clear that ego-consciousness still lived more or less in the atmosphere of Moon in the fire-mist, that it was still a part, a member, of a higher being, in whom existed all the egos which today are to be found in bodies separated by the skin one from another. As yet there were no human beings going about as they do today, equipped with ego-conscious-ness. On the other hand, however, something else was much more fully developed than on the earth.

You know that what is called folk-soul, race-soul, has become a somewhat abstract idea today. The individual soul of the human being that dwells in his body is considered by many today to be the actual reality. If one speaks of German, French, Russian nation-souls, people look on that as more or less an abstraction, as a comprehensive concept, embracing the characteristics which the individual members of those nations possess. To the spiritual researcher this is not so at all. What one calls the folk-soul, the German, French, Russian folk-soul, is to him an absolutely independent entity. It is only that in our present Earth existence the folk-soul is a purely spiritual being, perceptible only to one who can ascend to the astral plane; there you could not deny it, for there it is present as an actual living being. You would encounter the folk-soul there, as on the physical plane you encounter your friends.

On Moon it would have occurred to you even less to deny this group-soul, for at that time it had a still more real exist-ence. It was the folk-soul, the race-soul, which guided the bloodstream down into the bodies, into those beings which circled round Moon. It is the destiny of our age to deny the existence of such beings who live their real life on the astral plane and are not perceptible here on the physical plane. We are at the very height of this materialistic development which prefers to deny such beings as folk-souls and race-souls.

Recently a very characteristic book has appeared, which has been much advertised. It is a book that has been praised and is considered, quite rightly, to be a true expression of our abstract objective thinking, since it comes from the depths of the modern human soul. Such a book had to be written sooner or later. It denies everything that cannot be seen with the eyes or felt with the hands. It is a scandalous book from the standpoint of the spiritual researcher, a notable book, however, from the standpoint of present-day methods of thought. I refer to Mauthner's *Critique of Language*.[27] In this book a clean sweep is made of everything that cannot be grasped by the hand. Our age had to produce such a book as a kind of necessity. This is not meant as a criticism, it is only to point out the contrast between the esoteric mode of thought and the present time. You can find in it the exact opposite of all esoteric methods of thought; it is the most amazing product of a dying cultural stream of the present day, and from this point of view it is quite excellent.

You will understand that on Old Moon a more common consciousness prevailed than here on earth. On the earth human beings feel themselves to be individuals; on Moon this was not the case. On Moon the group-soul was active, which then appeared on the earth in a more attenuated form as the folk-soul; hence the whole Moon globe had a common consciousness in a high degree. This common consciousness on Moon felt itself to be feminine; and you know that Moon was irradiated by Sun, and Sun was experienced as masculine. This is preserved in old Egyptian myths; for instance the feminine Moon—Isis, and the masculine Sun—Osiris. An ego-consciousness enclosed in the human body was, however, altogether lacking. That was contained in the Moon atmosphere.

During the intermediate state between Moon and Earth, various beings worked in from the atmosphere of Moon, and made the human ether body and astral body ready to possess an ego-consciousness. What happened when Sun again shone forth still containing Moon and Earth within it? In the environment of this now newly awakened Sun-globe were the

beings who today form your souls, and during the intermediate stage they had incorporated ego-consciousness into
their astral and ether bodies. As yet the physical body did not
possess it, and indeed it once again emerged as the human-
animal it had been on Moon. Thus these two parts were no
longer in harmony. On Moon they had still harmonized, but
what had now descended into the astral and ether bodies was
no longer quite in harmony with what existed below as
physical body, and the consequence of this was that before a
harmony could arise the earlier states of Saturn, Sun and
Moon had to be recapitulated. Thus we have three recapitu-
lations before our actual Earth could appear.

First the Saturn existence came forth with the physical
bodies of the animal-humans, although in a certain respect no
longer as simple as they had been on Old Saturn. At that time
the sense organs had existed as rudimentary beginnings; now
the glandular and nerve organs were present in addition, but
they were incapable of taking in what was above. A short
recapitulation of Saturn existence had to take place. The
Spirits of Egohood and Independence had to work once more
on the physical bodies, in order to implant in them the power
of taking up the ego. In the same way the Sun-state had to be
passed through, so that these physical bodies, in respect of the
organs formed on Sun, could become capable of receiving an
ego. And in the same way the Moon condition was repeated in
order to make the nervous system fitted for it.

Thus there was first a kind of repetition of the Saturn stage.
In this the beings who had earlier been animal-humans now
moved about on Earth like automata or a kind of machine.
Then began the time when this repeated Saturn condition
went over into the Sun condition; there these human bodies
were like sleeping plants. Next came the repetition of the
Moon-state, where Sun had already extricated itself. Everything remained behind that had earlier already detached itself

as Moon. So once again the whole Moon-cycle was repeated, except that now the capacity to receive an ego was implanted into the beings.

This repetition of the Moon-cycle was for Earth, if one may say so, an evil period of its evolution, for considered spiritually, egohood had been implanted into the human being consisting of physical body, ether body and astral body, but without the purifying power of thought. During the time when Sun had already withdrawn and Earth had not yet cast out the moon, the human being was in a state in which his astral body was the bearer of the most savage lusts, for every bad force was implanted in him and there was no counterbalance. After the separation of Sun there was, to put it in today's language, a globe in which human beings were still entirely group-souls, but of the most sensual order and with the worst instincts.

During this passage through a veritable hell, and under the influence of the departed pure Sun forces (not only of the physical sun, but also of Sun-beings, who had withdrawn to the sun), the recapitulating Moon gradually matured so far that it could throw out the terrible instincts and powers, and retain on the earth whatever was capable of evolving. With the departure of the present moon all those sensual forces went away; therefore in the present moon you have the remains, also in its spiritual significance, of all the evil influences which were at that time present in the human realm; and therefore too the moon is looked upon as having a detrimental influence. Everything capable of evolution remained on the earth after the separation of the sun and moon.

Let us consider first the animal-humans themselves. They had gradually matured far enough for the ego to be incorporated. So we now have moving about on the earth human beings who consisted of four members (physical body, ether body, astral body and ego). For the first time the former swimming, floating position changed and they began gradually to achieve an upright posture. The spine and spinal cord became vertical, in contrast to the completely horizontal position they had maintained during the Moon period, and with this rise into an upright position came the widening out of the spinal cord into the brain. Yet another development also ran parallel with this. For the floating, swimming motion which human beings had both in the Moon period and during the repetition of that period when the fire-mist forces were still present in the environment, they needed a kind of buoyancy-bladder, and this was actually part of their composition, as is the case with fish of the present day. But now the fire-mist (we called it 'ruach') was precipitated out. This took place quite gradually and slowly. The air, to be sure, was still filled with thick vapour, but the worst was precipitated, and with this began the time when the human being changed from being a gill-breather to a lung-breather. The buoyancy-bladder was transformed into lungs. Through this human beings became capable of receiving into themselves the higher spiritual entities, namely the first rudiments of what is higher than the ego—the spirit-self or manas.

This metamorphosis of the buoyancy-bladder into the lungs is expressed in the Bible in the wonderful, monumental words: 'And God breathed into his nostrils the breath of life; and man became a living soul.'[28] This expresses what had been taking place in the human being over thousands of years.[29]

All the beings that we have come to know—the plant-animals as well as the animal-humans of Moon and their descendants during the Moon period of the earth—all of them still lacked red blood. What they possessed resembled the blood of present-day lower animals, which is not yet red. Blood-like substance flowed in and out of them from outside. In order to be able to harbour the red blood in themselves something else was necessary. We shall understand this when we know that until the casting out of the moon in the evolution of our planet no part had been played by iron. Until then there had been no iron on our planet; it received it when the planet Mars passed through our earth and, so to say, left iron behind. Hence the influence of iron in the red blood stems from Mars.

Legend has preserved this well by ascribing to Mars the qualities which iron brought to the blood—strong and warlike powers. Thus the influence which came in then, with the change in the breathing process, was supported by the introduction of iron into our organism. This was of the utmost importance in our terrestrial evolution. Under these influences the human organism became more complete. You could say that through the ego the human being began to purify and refine the bodies which he had earlier received on Saturn, Sun and Moon. He began to work first, of course, on the body that had been last received, the astral body, and this purification of the astral body constitutes our present culture and civilization.

If you could observe that human being, still in process of transformation towards lungs and taking the first steps towards the development of red blood, you would find him very unlike the present human form. He was so different that one really hesitates to describe him at that period, for it would appear grotesque to present-day materialistic thinkers. The human being had more or less developed into an amphibian, a reptile, which was just beginning to breathe with lungs, and from the former floating, swimming motion was learning little by little to raise and support himself on the earth. If we say that human beings in the Lemurian epoch moved in a way that alternated between a hop, scarcely to be called a step, and then a short flight in the air, we have the nearest approach to some memory of it in the old dinosaurs.[30] Nothing remains to be discovered by the geologist as solidifications or fossils, for the human body was quite soft, and it contained as yet no kind of bony structure.

How did the earth appear, after having freed itself from the moon? It had formerly been surrounded by fire-mists, as in a seething, steaming cauldron, and then by degrees the dense watery vapours withdrew. The earth was now covered by a very thin, hardened crust beneath which lay a bubbling, churning sea of fire, the remains of the fire-mist of the former atmosphere. Then gradually tiny islands emerged, the first beginnings of our present mineral kingdom. Whereas on Moon a plant-mineral kingdom had still existed, there now appeared the earliest foundations of our modern rocks and stones in consequence of the hardening, mineralizing of this mass. The animal-plant kingdom had also previously developed more or less into our present plant kingdom. And the beings on Moon who were animal-humans had divided into two groups, one of which had kept pace with evolution and taken on human form. But there were some who had not advanced with evolution; these are the present higher animals. They had stayed behind at an earlier level and since they could not share in the advance, they fell back more and more. All our present mammals are relics of the Moon animal-humans who stopped evolving. You must therefore never imagine that the human being was ever an animal such as those existing on the earth today. The bodies of these animals were not at that time capable of receiving the 'I', the ego; they had remained with the group-soul of Moon. The last of these which had almost managed to keep up and reach the Earth stage, but which nevertheless later on proved too weak to be the vehicle of an individual soul, are the apes, the present ape species. They too, however, were never actual ancestors of humanity, but beings which had degenerated.

In the Lemurian age the earth was a kind of fiery mass, in which the modern mineral element was for the most part liquefied and fluid, like iron in an iron-foundry today, and out of this developed the first mineral island mass. Upon this there moved, half hopping, half hovering, the forefathers of the human being. The spirit-self endeavoured little by little to gain possession of these human beings.

We must picture the ancient fiery period of the earth as a time in which a last echo still lingered of the forces of Moon, which then gradually disappeared. They were manifested in the mastery which the human will possessed over the substances and forces of nature. On Moon, of course, human beings had still been fully united with nature, and the group-soul had moulded the conditions of human existence. That was now no longer the case, but a magical connection between the human will and the forces of fire still continued. If a human being had a mild character, then, through the will, he acted on the natural element of fire in a calming manner, and in this way more land could be deposited. A passionate human being, on the other hand, worked with his will magically in such a way that the fire-masses became fierce and turbulent and tore open the thin earth crust. Once again the whole savage, passionate power that had been peculiar to human beings on Moon, and during the repetition of the Moon period on the earth, burst forth in the newly arisen individual human souls. The passions had such an effect on the fiery masses that they became ungovernable; a great part of the land on which the Lemurians dwelt was destroyed, and only a small number of the inhabitants of Lemuria were preserved and could continue the human race.

All of you were living in those times; your souls are the very ones which saved themselves from the raging fiery mass of Lemuria. The portion of humanity that saved itself migrated into the land we know as Atlantis, the main part of which stretches between the present Europe and America; from there the human race multiplied and spread. Gradually the earth's atmosphere had so changed that every trace of the old 'ruach' had gone, and the air was only saturated by dense masses of vapour. Germanic legend has preserved the memory of this in Niflheim or Nebelheim, a land permanently filled with similar heavy clouds of mist.

What had been working in from outside during the Lemurian age? At first, in Saturn, it was the beings whom we call the Spirits of Egoism, of the sense of independence. During Sun it was the archangels, the Fire-Spirits, and during Moon, those beings that were, so to speak, the good spirits of the Moon time, for which the Christian designation is angel, and which are called in theosophy Spirits of Twilight. We have designated the outstanding Leader of these spirits as the Holy Spirit or Holy Ghost, the Ruler of the Fire Spirits as the Christ, and of Saturn the Father God. Thus the last who had been at work with his hosts was the Spirit named in Christianity the Holy Spirit, the Ruler of the Moon-evolution, the Spirit who was still present during the earth's repetition of the Moon-period. It was the same Spirit who had formed the human being from without, and who now sent a ray of his own essence, so to say, into the human being. We have to distinguish two kinds of spirit in the beginning of the Lemurian age: the spirits who prepare the lower bodily nature, who implant ego-consciousness, who fashion the members of the human being, and that Spirit who actually entered into human beings at the moment they learned to breathe physically.

If you consider that everything which on Saturn formed a kind of fiery mass surrounded by a finer atmosphere, was gaseous on Sun, and then on Moon was surrounded by those masses of fire-mist, then you must regard the evolutionary process of Earth as one of purification, in the same way that the evolution of humanity itself is a purifying process. What one calls air today only gradually became free of all that filled it with a kind of steam and smoke. We must be clear that what separated itself out from the atmosphere are the substances from which all bodies have built themselves up. The air is the purest of what has remained behind. It is the best corporeal medium for the guiding Spirits of Moon, whom one calls angels in Christian terminology. Therefore in the purified air, in the air which had been refined, human beings felt the bodily nature of the new guiding spirits of the earth, the Spirit who now was the leader, Jehovah. In the stirring of the wind human beings experienced what it was that led and guided the earth. Thus they lived on into Atlantean times, on the continent that forms the present bed of the Atlantic Ocean, sensing in the breath which they drew the bodily nature of God.

The magical influence which human beings had had upon the fire-ocean, upon the processes of the earth, gradually disappeared, but in the early Atlantean age another connection remained instead. Human beings still possessed a degree of magical power over the growth of plants. If they held their hand, which at that time had quite a different shape, above a plant, they were able to make it grow more quickly through the influence of their will. They were still intimately related with the beings of nature. The whole life of the Atlanteans was in accordance with nature.

What we call the intelligence, the ability to think logically, to put two and two together, did not yet exist. On the other hand human beings had developed other capacities to a high degree, memory, for instance. Today we can scarcely imagine the fabulous degree of development this had attained. They could not calculate, not even that two times two makes four, but they knew the answer from memory; on each occasion they remembered the previous experience. Another aspect lingering into Atlantean times was that although human beings no longer felt the folk-soul directly within them as on Moon, they did experience the influence of the old folk-souls, race-souls. This influence was so strong that it would have been quite impossible in those times for anyone who belonged to one race or folk-soul ever to unite with one who belonged to another race. There was a deep antipathy between the peoples of the various folk-souls; love only existed between those belonging to the same one. We may say that the common blood, which earlier in the Moon period had been poured down from the folk-soul, was the basis of this kinship. Human beings remembered—not only in some dim way, but quite clearly—the experiences of their forefathers. They felt themselves linked by their common blood in the chain of ancestry just as you feel your hand to be an item belonging to your organism. This feeling of kinship was a part of evolution inasmuch as, in the transitionary period we have been considering which took place when the sun withdrew and the moon was cast out, another important event took place. It is connected with all that was proceeding on the earth as a sort of hardening process. The mineral kingdom appeared and at the same time a similar hardening also took place in the interior of human nature. Something more solid formed itself by degrees out of the soft mass, and hardened first to cartilage and then to bone. Not until the skeletal structure was formed did the walking movement of human beings begin.

Another process ran parallel with the shaping of the skeleton. In consequence of the advance of human evolution brought about by the casting out of the moon and the retention only of what was able to develop, two different forces arose in the beings inhabiting the earth. Both the sun and the moon were now outside and their influences affected the earth from without. From this intermingling of the sun-forces and the moon-forces, which had previously been in the body of the earth, but now streamed in from without, sexual life made its appearance. All the forces connected with sexuality come under the influence of the sun and moon forces.

From this point of view, the still united sun, moon and earth of ancient times could be looked on as female, and this was fructified, so to say, by the forces of the sun itself. The sun experienced itself as male, the moon as female. Now the moon withdrew, and the forces of both mingled. In a general way we can describe all the beings that arose up to the departure of the moon as being of a female nature, for all the fructifying forces came from without, from the sun-force. Only upon an earth which had cast out the moon, so that the sun shone upon quite a different cosmic body, could the former undifferentiated female divide into male and female. Along with the solidifying, bone-forming process, therefore, the differentiation into sexes took place. Thus the possibility of perfecting the ego in the right way came about.

# Lecture 12

# The Evolution of Humanity on the Earth II

The process that I have described to you as the division of the sexes was of such a nature that the two sexes are to be thought of as still united in that animal-human of Moon and also in its descendants in the Moon recapitulation of Earth. After this a kind of division of the human body really did take place. This division came about through a kind of densification; not until a mineral kingdom had been separated out as it is today could the present human body arise, representing a single sex. The earth and the human body first had to be solidified to the mineral nature as we know it. In the soft human bodies of Moon and the first period of Earth, human beings were of dual sex, male-female.

We must remind ourselves that in a certain respect the human being has preserved a residue of this ancient dual sex, since in the present man the physical body is male and the ether body female, while in the woman this is reversed; the female physical body today has a masculine ether body. These facts open up an interesting insight into the soul life of the sexes. The capacity for sacrifice in the service of love displayed by the woman is connected with the masculinity of her ether body, whereas ambition in the man is explained when we realize the female nature of his ether body.

I have already said that separation into the human sexes arose from the intermingling of the forces sent to us from the sun and moon. In this connection you must understand that in the man the stronger influence on the ether body emanates from the moon and the stronger influence on the physical body from the sun. In the woman the opposite is the case; her physical body is influenced by forces of the moon and her ether body by those of the sun.

The continual exchange of mineral substances in the human being's present body could not come about until the mineral realm had taken shape; before that there was quite a different form of nourishment. During Earth's Sun period all plants were full of milky juices. Human beings were nourished by imbibing the milky juices from the plants as today the child draws nourishment from its mother. The plants which still contain milky juices are the last stragglers from the time when all plants supplied these juices in abundance. It was not until a later time that nourishment took on its present form.

To understand the significance of the separation of the sexes we must be clear that upon Moon and during its recapitulation on the earth all the beings looked very much alike. Just as a cow has much the same appearance as her descendants and all other cows, since the group-soul is in the background, so could human beings scarcely be distinguished from their forefathers, and this continued until well into the Atlantean age.

Why is it that human beings no longer resemble each other? It comes from the establishment of the two sexes. From the original androgynous nature the tendency has continued in the female to produce similarity in the descendants. In the male the influence worked differently; it tended to call forth variety, individualization, and with the flowing of the male force into the female, dissimilarity was increasingly created. Thus it was through the male influence that the power of developing individuality came about.

The ancient dual sex had yet another peculiarity. If you had asked one of the old dwellers on Moon about his experiences, he would have described them as identical with those of his earliest ancestors; everything lived on through the generations. The gradual rise of a consciousness that only extends from birth to death came about through the individualizing of the human race, and at the same time arose the possibility of birth and death as we know them today. Those ancient Moon beings with their floating, swimming motion were suspended from the environment into which they sent the 'strings' conducting their blood. Thus if a being died it was not a death of the soul, it was only a dying off of a sort of limb, while the consciousness remained above. It was as if your hand, for instance, were to wither on your body and a new hand grow in its place. Thus these human beings with their dim consciousness experienced dying merely as a gradual withering of their bodies. These bodies dried up and new ones continually sprouted out. Consciousness, however, was preserved through the consciousness of the group-soul, so that a kind of immortality really existed.

Then the present blood came into being, created in the human body itself, and this went hand in hand with the arrival of the two sexes. With this a remarkable process became necessary. The blood creates a continuous conflict between life and death. A being that forms red blood within itself becomes the scene of a perpetual struggle, for red blood is continually used up and changed into blue blood, into the substance of death. Together with the human being's individual transformation of the blood arose that darkening of consciousness beyond birth and death. Now, for the first time, with the lighting up of the present consciousness, the human being lost the ancient, dimly-sensed immortality, so that the impossibility of looking beyond birth and death is intimately connected with the division of the sexes. Something else, too, is connected with this.

When the human being still possessed a group-soul, existence went on from generation to generation, with no interruption being caused through birth and death. Then this interruption appeared and with it the possibility of reincarnation. Earlier, the son was merely a direct continuation of the father, the father of the grandfather; consciousness did not break off. Now there came a time when consciousness was dimmed beyond birth and death, and a sojourn in kamaloca and Devachan first became possible. This interchange, this sojourn in higher worlds, could only come about at all after the individualization, after the expulsion of sun and moon. Only then did incarnation, as we call it, come about, and at the same time this intermediate state, which will one day also come to an end again.

We have reached the period at which the earlier androgynous organism, representing a kind of group-soul, divided into a male and a female in such a way that the similar is reproduced through the female and the varied and dissimilar through the male. We see in our stage of evolution the female as the principle which still preserves the old conditions of folk and race, and the male that which continually breaks through these conditions, splits them up and so individualizes humanity. There is at work in the human being an ancient female principle as group-soul and a new male principle as an individualizing element. Eventually all connections of race and family stock will cease to exist; human beings will become more and more different from one another. Interrelationship will no longer depend on the common blood but only on what binds soul to soul. That is the course of human evolution.

In the first Atlantean races there still existed a strong bond of union and the first sub-races grouped themselves according to their colouring. We still have this group-soul element in the races of different colour. These differences will increasingly disappear as the individualizing element gains the upper hand. A time will come when there will no longer be races of different colour; the difference between the races will have disappeared, but on the other hand there will be the greatest differences between individuals. The further we go back into ancient times, the more we meet with the prevalance of the racial element. The truly individualizing principle only began as a whole in later Atlantean times. Among the earlier Atlanteans, members of one race actually experienced a deep antipathy for members of another, whereas common blood caused a feeling of connection, of love. It was considered improper to marry a member of another stock.

If, as a seer, you were to examine the connection between the ether body and the physical body in the old Atlanteans you would make a remarkable discovery. Whereas in the human being of today the etheric head virtually coincides with the physical part of the head and only protrudes slightly beyond it, in the old Atlantean the etheric head projected well beyond the physical head. In particular it protruded strongly in the region of the forehead. Think of a point in the physical brain in the place between the eyebrows, but about a centimetre lower, and a second point in the etheric head corresponding to this. In the Atlanteans these two points were still far apart, and evolution consisted precisely in the fact that they gradually came closer together. In the fifth Atlantean period the point in the etheric head moved into the physical brain, and by reason of these two points coming together there developed what we possess today: calculation, counting, the capacity to judge, the power of forming ideas in general, intelligence. Formerly the Atlanteans had only an immensely developed memory, but as yet no logical intellect. Here we have the point at which the ego began to grow conscious.

A self-reliant independence did not exist in the Atlanteans before these two points coincided; on the other hand they were able to live in a much more intimate contact with nature. Their dwellings were constructed out of what was given by nature; they moulded the stones and bound them together with the growing trees. Their dwellings were formed out of living nature, were really transformed natural objects. They lived in little tribes that were still preserved through blood relationship, whilst a powerful authority was exercised by the strongest, who was the chieftain. Everything depended on authority, which was exercised, however, in a way peculiar to those times.

When human beings entered the Atlantean age, they could not yet utter articulate speech; this was only developed during that period. A chieftain could not have given commands in speech, but on the other hand these human beings had the faculty of understanding the language of nature. Present day human beings have no idea of this, they have to learn it anew. Imagine, for instance, a spring of water which reflects your image to you. As a spiritual researcher a peculiar feeling emerges in your soul. You say: My image comes towards me out of this spring; to me this is a last token of how on old Saturn everything was reflected out into space. The memory of Saturn arises in the researcher when he sees his reflection in the spring. Likewise in the echo which gives back the spoken sound there arises the recollection of how on Saturn all that resounded into cosmic space came back as an echo. Or you see a *fata morgana*, a mirage in the air, in which the air seems to have taken up whatever pictures are imprinted in it and then reflects them again. As a spiritual researcher you see here a memory of the Sun period, when the gaseous Sun took in all that came to it from cosmic space, worked it over, and then let it stream back, giving it its own sun-nature at the same time. On the Sun planet you would have seen how things were prepared as a *fata morgana*, a kind of mirage within the gases of the Sun incarnation. In this way, without being a magician, one learns to grasp the world from many aspects, and that is an important means towards developing into higher worlds.

In ancient times human beings understood nature to a higher degree. There is a great difference between living in an atmosphere like the present or one such as that in Atlantis.

The air then was saturated with immense vapour masses; sun and moon were surrounded by a gigantic rainbow halo. There was a time when the mist-masses were so dense that no eye could have seen the stars, when sun and moon were still darkened. Only gradually did they become visible to human beings. This coming into sight of sun, moon and stars is magnificently described in records of the Creation. What is described there really did take place, and much more besides.

The Atlanteans still had a strong understanding of their natural environment. All that sounds in the rippling of the spring, in the windy storm, and is an inarticulate sound to you today, was heard by the Atlanteans as speech they could understand. There were at that time no commandments, but the spirit pierced through the vapour-drenched air and spoke to the human being. The Bible expresses this in the words: 'And the Spirit of God moved upon the face of the waters.'[31] Human beings heard the spirit from surrounding objects; from sun, moon and stars the spirit spoke to them, and you find in those words in the Bible a plain expression for what took place in their environment.

Then came the time in which an especially advanced portion of the human race, who lived in a region which today is on the bed of the ocean in the neighbourhood of present Ireland, first experienced that definite union with the ether body and thus an increase of intelligence. This portion of humanity began to journey eastwards under the guidance of those most advanced while gradually immense volumes of water submerged the continent of Atlantis. The most advanced portion of these people journeyed right into Asia, and there founded the centre of those civilizations that we call post-Atlantean culture. From this centre civilization radiated out; it proceeded from the groups of people who later moved further to the east. There in Central Asia they founded in India the first of these civilizations, which still had a strong echo of the culture attained in Atlantis. The ancient Indians did not yet have a consciousness like that of today, but the capacity for it arose when those two points of the brain I mentioned coincided. Before this union there still lived a picture-consciousness in the Atlanteans, through which they saw spiritual beings. In the murmuring of the fountain they not only heard a clear language, but the Undine, who has her embodiment in the water, rose for them out of the spring; in the currents of air they saw Sylphs; in the flickering fire they saw the Salamanders. All this they saw and from it have arisen the myths and legends that have been preserved with most purity in the parts of Europe where there remained remnants of those Atlanteans who did not reach India. The Germanic sagas and myths are the relics of what was still seen by the old Atlanteans within the vapoury masses. The rivers, the Rhine for instance, lived in the consciousness of those old Atlanteans as if the wisdom which was in the mists of ancient Niflheim had precipitated out in their waters. This wisdom seemed to them to be in the rivers; it lived there in the form of Rhine nymphs or similar beings.

Here in these regions of Europe lived echoes of Atlantean culture, but over in India another culture arose, one that still showed remembrances of that picture world. That world itself had sunk from sight, but the longing for what was revealed in it lived on in the Indian. While the Atlantean had heard the voice of nature's wisdom, to the Indian there remained a longing for oneness with nature, and thus the character of this old Indian culture is shown in the desire to return to that time when all this was the human being's natural possession. The ancient Indian was a dreamer. To be sure, what we call reality lay spread out all around him, but the world of the senses was *maya* in his eyes. What the old Atlantean still saw as hovering spirits was what the Indian sought in his longing for the spiritual content of the world, for Brahma. This kind of going back towards the old dream-like consciousness of the Atlantean has been preserved in oriental training as a way of retrieving this early consciousness.

Further to the north we have the Medes and Persians, the original Persian civilization. Whereas the Indian culture turns sharply away from reality, the Persian is aware that he must reckon with it. For the first time the human being appears as a worker, who knows that he has not merely to strive for knowledge with his spiritual forces, but that he has to use them for shaping the earth. At first the earth met him as a sort of hostile element which he must overcome, and this opposition was expressed in Ormuzd and Ahriman, a good and an evil divinity, and the conflict between them. People wished more and more to let the spiritual world flow into the terrestrial world, but as yet they could recognize no law, no laws of nature within the outer world. The old Indian culture had a genuine knowledge of higher worlds, but not based on a knowledge of nature, since everything on the earth was accounted *maya*; the Persian learnt to know nature purely as a place of work.

Then we come to the Chaldean, the Babylonian and the Egyptian peoples. Here people learnt to recognize a law in nature itself. When they looked up to the stars they sought behind them not the gods alone, but they examined the laws of the stars, and hence arose that wonderful science which we find among the Chaldeans. The Egyptian priest did not look on the physical as an opposing force, but he incorporated the spiritual which he found in geometry into his soil, his land; outer nature was recognized as conforming to laws. In Chaldean-Babylonian-Egyptian wisdom, external star-knowledge was inwardly united with knowledge of the gods who ensoul the stars. That was the third stage of cultural evolution.

It was only in the fourth stage of post-Atlantean evolution

that human beings advanced to the point of incorporating in civilization what they themselves experienced as spiritual. This is what occurred in the Greco-Latin time. Here, in works of art, in moulded matter, human beings imprinted their own spirit into substance, whether in sculpture or in drama. Here too we find the first beginnings of city planning by human beings. These cities differed from those of Egypt in the pre-Grecian age. In Egypt the priests looked up to the stars and sought their laws, and what took place in the heavens they reproduced in what they built. Thus their towers show the seven-stepped development which human beings first discovered in the heavenly bodies; so too do the pyramids show definite cosmic proportions.

We find the transition from priest-wisdom to real human wisdom wonderfully expressed in early Roman history by the seven Kings of Rome. What are these seven kings? We remember that the original history of Rome leads back to ancient Troy. Troy represents a last result of the ancient priestly communities who organized states according to the laws of the stars. Now came the transition to the fourth stage of culture. Ancient priest-wisdom was superseded by human cleverness, represented by the crafty Odysseus. Still more plainly is this shown in a picture which can only be rightly understood in this way and which represents how the priest-wisdom had to give way before the human power of judgement. The serpent can always be taken as a symbol of human wisdom, and the Laocoon group depicts the overthrow of the priestly wisdom of ancient Troy through human cunning and human wisdom symbolized in the serpents.[32]

By the directing powers who work through millennia the events were then outlined that had to happen and in accordance with which history must take its course. Those who stood at the foundation of Rome had already pre-ordained the sevenfold Roman culture as written in the

Sibylline Books. Think it through yourselves. You find in the names of the seven Roman kings reminiscences of the seven principles of the human being. This goes so far, in fact, that the fifth Roman king, the Etruscan, comes from outside; he represents the principle of manas, spirit-self, which links the three lower and the three higher principles. The seven Roman kings represent the seven principles of human nature; spiritual connections are inscribed in them. Republican Rome was nothing other than human wisdom replacing ancient priestly wisdom. In this way the fourth age grew out of the third. Human beings sent forth what they had in their soul into the great works of art, into drama and jurisprudence. Formerly all justice had been derived from the stars. The Romans became a nation of law-givers because there human beings created jurisprudence according to their own requirements.

We ourselves live in the fifth period. How does the meaning of overall evolution come to expression in it? The old authority has vanished, human beings become more and more dependent on their own inner nature, their external acts increasingly bear the stamp of their own character. Racial ties lose their hold, people become more and more individualized. This is the kernel of the religion which says: He who does not forsake father and mother, brothers and sisters, cannot be my disciple.[33] This means that all love which is founded on natural ties alone must come to an end; human beings must approach one another, and soul find soul.

We have the task of drawing down still further on to the physical plane what flowed from the soul in Greco-Latin times. In this way human beings sink deeper and deeper into materiality. Whilst the Greeks in their works of art created an idealized image of their soul-life and poured it into the human form, whilst the Romans with their jurisprudence created something that still further signified personal requirements, our age culminates in machines that are an entirely materialistic expression of mere personal human needs. Humanity has descended further and further away from heaven, and in this fifth period has arrived at the deepest point, where it is now most strongly ensnared in matter. Whilst the Greeks in their creations raised the human being above himself in their images (for Zeus represents the human being raised above himself), whilst you still find in Roman jurisprudence something of the human being that goes beyond himself (for the Roman placed more value on being a Roman citizen than on being a person and an individual), in our period you find people who utilize spirit for the satisfaction of their material needs. For what purpose is served by all machines, steamships, railways, all complicated inventions? The ancient Chaldean was accustomed to satisfy his need for food in the simplest way; today an immensity of wisdom, crystallized human wisdom, is expended on the quenching of hunger and thirst. We must not deceive ourselves about this. The wisdom that is so employed has descended below itself right into matter.

All that human beings had earlier drawn down from the spiritual realms had to descend below itself in order to be able to mount upwards again—and with this our age has received its mission. Whilst in human beings of an earlier time there flowed the blood which bound them to their tribe, today the love which still flowed in the earlier blood is becoming more and more fragmented. A love of a spiritual kind must take its place and then we can ascend again to spiritual realms. There is good reason for us to have come down from spiritual heights, for the human being must go through this descent in order to find the way up to spirituality out of his own strength. It is the mission of spiritual science to show humanity this upward path.

We have followed the course of humanity as far as the time

in which we ourselves are. We must now show how it will evolve further, and how one who passes through an initiation can even today anticipate a specific stage of humanity on its further path of knowledge and wisdom.

# The Future of Humanity

Our task today is to mention a few aspects of the progress of human evolution in the future, and of what is called initiation. It is by means of initiation that present-day human beings can pass in advance through stages of life which are otherwise only to be passed through by humanity in the future.

With regard to the first question, you may think it audacious to try and speak about the future, or even that it is impossible to find out anything about the future of the human being. Nevertheless, if you consider the matter a little you will find the idea of knowing something about the future not so unfounded after all. You need only compare this with what the ordinary researcher, the scientist, for example, can know with regard to future events. He can tell you definitely that if he mixes oxygen, hydrogen and sulphur under certain conditions, sulphuric acid always results. You can say exactly what will happen when you intercept rays by a mirror. In fact, with regard to external life you can go even further, for you can predict eclipses of the sun and moon over indefinitely long periods of time.

How is it possible to do this? It can be done because and in so far as you know the laws of physical life. So if someone knows the spiritual laws of life, from these laws he can likewise say what must come about in the future. Here, however, a question generally arises which weighs heavily on people's minds. It is so easy to imagine that it would be a contradiction of freedom, of people's own voluntary acts, if it could be known in advance what will happen. This is an incorrect idea. When you combine sulphur, hydrogen and oxygen under certain conditions, sulphuric acid arises; that is determined by the laws of combination. Whether you do it, however, depends on your will; and so it is also in the spiritual course of human evolution. What will happen will be done by human beings in entire freedom of will, and the higher an individual develops, the freer he will be. You must not think that it is already decided what an individual will do in the future merely because one can see it in advance. Most people, however, have no correct understanding of this problem and in fact it presents very great difficulties. Since ancient times philosophers have tormented themselves with the question of human freedom and the law of predestined phenomena. Practically all that has been written in this field is extremely unsatisfactory, for as a rule people cannot distinguish between foreseeing and being preordained. Seeing in advance is in fact no different from looking out to some distant spot. If you look to a point some way off, let us say the corner of the street over there, and you see a person giving a penny to someone, have you brought about this action? Has it been caused through the fact that you see it? No, you only see that he does it, and that exercises no pressure on his act.

In a certain respect the situation is the same in the case of time, only people cannot grasp it. Let us suppose you are reincarnated in a couple of thousand years, and you then do something of your own free will; that is the same as the example of the gift of the penny. Under certain circumstances the seer sees what is done in the future, yet this future act is just as little determined by the present point in time as the gift of the penny by the point in space. People often say: If one sees that something will happen it must be predetermined. But then one is confounding the present with the future. In fact it would be no prevision into the future if it were already predestined; you are not seeing something that is already there, but something that will come. You must accurately grasp the concept of seeing-into-the-future. You must exercise and practise this in patient meditation; only then does one find it possible to understand these things correctly.

After these introductory words we will now mention a few things about the evolution of humanity in the future. We have today reached the point where humanity has descended most deeply into matter, where human beings apply their spiritual forces to the construction and manufacture of instruments and machines that serve their personal life. Connected with this there has been an ever-increasing densification, both of the human being and the earth as a whole. We have seen that the mineral kingdom, as we call it, the densest part of the earth, only arose at a definite point of time in our evolution. It was only then that the human being entered upon his present earthly development; and the division of the sexes and other phenomena went hand in hand with that. At the time when the human being had not as yet entered this physical development which contains a mineral kingdom, he was still of a much finer, softer nature. To gain some idea of this, consider how the reproduction of the human race took place in those ancient times before the two sexes were in existence. At that time the human being, who was still androgynous and of a less dense, finer corporeality, brought forth another being from within. Reproduction was not as it is today, but rather like in spiritualist séances, when the ether body of some other being proceeds from the medium. That gives you more or less a picture of this materialization from oneself, the manner of human reproduction in ancient times. It was like a pressing-out from human beings who were ready to continue their own development.

Thus you see that a descent into the world of matter is connected with the densification of the human being in the cosmos. There is also another force connected with it, which could never have developed without it: egoism. Egoism has a good and a bad side. It is the foundation of human independence and freedom, but in its reverse aspect the foundation, too, of all that is bad and evil. But human beings had to go through this force of egoism if they were to learn to do good out of their own free will. Through the forces that had guided them previously, they would always have been impelled to the good; however, they needed the possibility of going their own way. Just as they have descended they must now ascend again to spirituality; and as the descent is linked with the predominance of egoism, so does the ascent depend on the selflessness of human beings, their feeling of sympathy for one another becoming stronger and stronger. Humanity has evolved through various epochs, first through the old Indian, then the Persian, the Egyptian-Chaldean-Babylonian, the Greco-Latin to the present, the fifth epoch. This in due course will be followed by a sixth. As human evolution is working towards this, it is at the same time working at overcoming the principle that has been strongest since the time when the ether body united with the point in the brain of which I spoke to you yesterday. That was the time of the fall into the deepest egoism.

The human being was egoistic in his earlier evolution too, but in a different way. The egoism that enters so deeply into the soul in our present age is inseparable from the predominating materialism of our age; a spiritual age will denote the overcoming of this egoism. Therefore Christianity and all movements imbued with genuine religious life have worked consciously towards breaking through all the old blood-ties. Christianity has made a radical statement in the words: He who does not forsake father, mother, wife, child, brother, sister, cannot be my disciple.[33] This indicates nothing less than that in place of the ancient blood ties there must enter the spiritual bond between soul and soul, between one human individual and another.

The only question now is: What are the ways and means by which humanity may attain spirituality, that is, the over-coming of materialism, and at the same time reach what may be called the bond of brotherhood, the expression of universal human love? One might imagine that universal human love need only be stressed strongly enough, and that then it must come about; or that one should found fraternities which aim at the goal of a universal human love. Spiritual science is never of this opinion. On the contrary! The more people speak of universal brotherly love and humanity, becoming in a sense intoxicated by these, the more egoistic they become. For like a lust of the senses there is also a lust of the soul. It is in fact a refined voluptuousness to say: I will become morally higher and higher. Although this thought does not lead to ordinary conventional egoism, it does lead to a subtle form of egoism arising from such voluptuousness.

It is not by emphasizing 'love' or 'sympathy' that these are generated in the course of human evolution. Humanity is much more likely to be led to that bond of brotherhood by something else, namely by spiritual knowledge itself. There is no other means of bringing about a universal human brother-hood than the spreading of esoteric knowledge through the world. One may talk for ever of Love and the Brotherhood of Mankind, one may found thousands of fraternities; they will not lead to the desired goal, however well-intentioned they may be. The point is to use the right means, to know how to found this bond of brotherhood and sisterhood. Only those whose lives are grounded in universal esoteric truth, valid for all human beings, find themselves together in the one truth. As the sun unites the plants which strive towards it while yet remaining individually separate, so must the truth to which all are striving be a uniform one; then all human beings will come together. But they must work energetically towards truth, for only then can they live together in harmony.

You might object that surely all are striving towards the truth, but that there are different standpoints, and therefore strife and dissensions arise. This denotes an insufficiently thorough knowledge of truth. One must not plead that there may be different standpoints; one must first experience that truth is single and indivisible. It does not depend on popular vote; it is true in itself. Or would you put it to the vote as to whether the three angles of a triangle add up to 180 degrees? Whether millions of people agree about this, or not a single one, when you have recognized it, it is true for you. There is no democracy about truth. Those who are not yet in harmony have not penetrated far enough into the truth, and this is the origin of all dispute over truth. You might say: Yes, but one person asserts this and another that in esoteric matters! In genuine esotericism that is not so. It is the same in esoteric things as in materialistic things; there, too, someone asserts this and another that, but then one of them is wrong. It is the same with genuine esotericism; but people often have a bad habit of judging esoteric matters before they have understood them.

The aim of the sixth epoch of humanity will be to popularize esoteric truth in the widest circles; that is the mission of that epoch. A society which is united in spirit has the task of carrying this esoteric truth everywhere—right into life—and applying it practically. This is precisely what is lacking in our age. Only look how our epoch is searching and how no one can find the right solution. There are innumerable problems, the education problem, women's suffrage, medicine, the social problem, the food question. People chip away at these problems, endless articles are written, and each talks from his or her own standpoint, without being willing to study the esoteric truth that lies at the centre.

It is not a matter of having some abstract knowledge of the truths of spiritual science, but of applying them directly to life, of studying the social problem, the education problem, in fact the whole range of human life, from the standpoint of real esoteric wisdom. 'But then,' it might be urged, 'one would have to know the highest wisdom.' This arises from the mistake of thinking one must always understand what one makes use of in life. But that is not necessary; understanding of the highest principles often comes much later than their application. If humanity had wished to wait in the matter of digestion until the laws of digestion were understood, then the evolution of humanity would not have been possible. So, too, one does not need to be aware of all spiritual laws in order to let spiritual science flow into everyday life. It is not a matter of saying spiritual science is spiritual science, but of taking spiritual science seriously in everyday life. That is precisely the way in which the Rosicrucian method deals with the spiritual—fewer abstractions, but instead the study of the problems of everyday life. Do you think that the child knows all the grammatical rules of speech once it has learnt to speak? First it learns to speak and then it learns grammar. So we must stress the value of using spiritual teachings to broach what lies directly around us, before occupying ourselves with what is to be found in the highest worlds, with information concerning the astral plane and Devachan. This is the only way to understand what exists in our surroundings, and where we ourselves must play our part. We shall find that it is our task to bind together through the unifying bonds of spiritual wisdom those portions of humanity which have been extricated from the old bonds of blood and race.

Then, inasmuch as we evolve from the fifth into the sixth and then into the seventh epoch, the ancient connections of race and blood will be increasingly lost. Humanity will become freer of physical ties in order to form groups from the aspect of the spirit. It was a bad habit in theosophy to speak of races as if they would always remain. The concept of race will lose its meaning in the near future, which means over the next few thousand years.[34] To state incessantly that seven and again seven races have always evolved in the world is the speculative extension of an idea that only holds good for our age—looking backwards and forwards; it has never been said from clairvoyant vision, from esoteric wisdom. Races have arisen, as everything else arises; and as everything dies out again, so will races die out too. Those who have always spoken of races will have to accustom themselves to making their ideas more fluid; not to do so is merely lazy. If you only look a little way into the future you find that ideas applied to the past and present are already no longer valid. It is most important that people should not consider that something they have once brought into a beautiful concept is a truth for all time. People must get into the habit of making ideas fluid, of recognizing that ideas change—that will be an advance. The ability of passing over from rigidly dogmatic ideas to fluid and flexible ones must be cultivated in those who would be the bearers of the future. For just as times change so must our ideas change too, if we would understand the times.

The soul now lives in a human body which you perceive distinctly with your senses. By what means has it arisen? It was very different in earlier times when the soul descended; in fact, for our present material outlook the difference is even comical. The soul took up its abode in the body. By what means has the human body evolved to its present form? By means of the soul itself working in the body during all its incarnations. You can form an idea of how the soul has worked on the body if you consider what possibility has remained to us today in this materialistic age for working on our body. We can now work relatively little on our dense physical body. Look at the way you temporarily affect your body and its physiognomy. For instance something gives you a fright or makes you anxious; the impression of anxiety or fear makes you turn pale. Your physical appearance is also affected by the blush of shame or embarrassment. It passes away again, but you see how it is caused. Something acts on the soul and the effects extend to the blood and thence to the physical body, changing its very appearance. The effect can be still more intensive. You know that people who lead a life of thought have it very much in their power to create an impression on their countenance of their intellectual work. You can observe whether or not someone has lived a life of mental activity. So people do still work on their external expression, and someone with noble feelings displays them in dignified movements. These are only slight remnants of how human beings have worked on themselves over thousands of years.[35]

Whereas nowadays you can only bring blood to your cheeks and drive it away again, in earlier times human beings were entirely under the influence of a picture-world which was the expression of a world of spirit. The effect of this influence was that the human being could work much more creatively on his body, and the body was also more soft and yielding. There was a time when you could not merely stretch out your hand, when you could not only point with your finger, but when you could send your will into your hand, and so form it that you could thrust out fingers as extensions. There was a time when feet were not yet permanent but could be pushed out as extensions when the human being needed them. Thus through the pictures which he received from the surrounding world the human being shaped his own body. Today in our material age this moulding is unimaginably slow, but a time will come again when it will proceed more rapidly. In the future human beings will again acquire more influence over their physical bodies. We shall see when we consider initiation by what means they will gain this influence. Although they may not reach it in one lifetime, yet they will be able to do much for the next incarnation.

Thus human beings themselves will bring about the future shape of their bodies. Inasmuch as they become softer and softer, inasmuch as they separate themselves from the hard part, they will be approaching their future. An age will come when they will live above their earthly part, as was the case in times gone by. This condition, which is comparable to your present sleep-condition, will then be replaced by another when the human being will be able to draw his ether body out of his physical body at will. It will be as if the denser part were here below on earth while the human being makes use of it from outside like an instrument. Human beings will no longer carry their bodies about and live within them, but will float above them; the bodies themselves will have become rarefied and more delicate. This seems fantastic now, but one can be distinctly aware of it from spiritual laws, just as one can calculate future eclipses of the sun and moon from the laws of astronomy.

Above all it will be upon the reproductive force that the human being will work. He will transform it. Many people cannot imagine that there will ever be a different reproductive process. But it will be so; the process of reproduction will be altered. The reproductive process and all that is connected with it will pass in the future to another organ. The organ that is already preparing to become the future organ of reproduction is the human larynx. Today it can only bring forth vibrations of the air, can only impart to the air what lies in a word that goes forth from it, so that the vibrations correspond to the word. Later on, not only will the word press forward in its rhythm from the larynx, but it will be irradiated by the human being, it will be suffused by substance itself. Just as today the word only becomes air waves, so in the future the person's inner being, his own likeness, which today is in his word, will issue from the larynx. The human being will proceed from the human being, the human being will speak forth the human being. This in the future will be how a new human being is born—by being spoken forth by another.

Such things throw a specific light on phenomena in our surroundings which no ordinary science can explain. The transformation of reproduction, which will once again be non-sexual, will supersede the previous manner of reproduction. That is why in the male organism at the age of puberty a change also takes place in the larynx, making the voice deeper. This is a direct indication of how these two things are interconnected. Thus spiritual wisdom throws light again and again on facts of life and illumines phenomena for which materialistic science can give you no explanation.

Just as the larynx will be transformed, so too will the human heart. It is the organ which has an intimate connection with the circulation. Science believes that the heart is a kind of pump. This is a grotesquely fantastic idea. Esoteric wisdom has never made statements as fantastic as those of modern materialism. It is the feelings of the soul which give rise to the movement of the blood; the soul drives the blood, and the heart moves because it in turn is driven by the blood. The truth is thus the exact opposite of what materialistic science states. Today, however, we cannot guide our heart at will. When we feel anxious it beats faster, since the feeling acts on the blood, and this quickens the motion of the heart. But what is suffered involuntarily by people today will later on, at a higher stage of evolution, be in their own power. Later on they will drive their blood by their own volition, and cause the movement of their heart as today they move the muscles of their hands. The heart with its peculiar structure is a crux, a riddle for modern science. It has striated muscle fibres, which are otherwise only to be found in voluntary muscles.[36] Why? Because the heart has not yet reached the end of its evolution, but is an organ of the future; because it will in the future be a voluntary muscle. Thus it already shows the rudiments of this in its structure.

All that goes on in the soul changes the organism. Imagine someone who is able to create his own likeness through the spoken word, whose heart has become a voluntary muscle, who will have altered yet other organs. Then you have a conception of the future of the human race in future planetary incarnations of Earth. Humanity will progress on our earth as far as it is possible under the influence of the mineral kingdom. This mineral kingdom, in spite of having arisen the last, will be the first to disappear again in its present form. The human being will then no longer build up his body from mineral substances as today. The coming human body will only incorporate into itself substances of a plant nature. All that works in the human being today as mineral will disappear. Here is a seemingly grotesque example: today we spit out our ordinary saliva. It is a mineral product, for the physical body is an interaction of mineral processes. When human beings have ended their mineral evolution they will no longer have mineral spittle; it will be of a plant nature—people will, so to speak, spit flowers. Glands will no longer secrete what is mineral, but only a vegetable substance. The mineral kingdom will be brought to an end by the evolutionary return of humanity to vegetable, plant existence.

Thus the human being will pass on to Jupiter by expelling all that is mineral and progressing to the creativeness of the plant. Later still he will pass over to animal-creativeness—animals will be different from those of today—when his heart will have progressed so far that it can appear as a creator. Then the human being will create in the animal world as today he creates in the mineral kingdom; this is when the Venus incarnation will arise. When the human being can create his kind by virtue of uttering his own likeness, then will the meaning of evolution be complete, then will the words be fulfilled: 'Let us make man in our image, after our likeness.'[37]

Only by observing this aspect—that the body will be

moulded by the soul—will the human being really transform the human race. Only through a thinking trained in the esoteric and spiritual sense will there appear what has been described as the transformation of the heart and the larynx. What humanity thinks today, that will it be in the future. A humanity that thinks materialistically will produce frightful beings in the future, and a humanity that thinks spiritual thoughts will work in such a way upon the future organism, transforming it, that beautiful human bodies will proceed from it.

What the materialistic mode of thought brings about has not yet been completed. We have two streams today, a great materialistic one which fills the earth, and a small spiritual one which is restricted to only a few human beings. Distinguish between soul-evolution and race-evolution. Do not think that if races pass over to a grotesque form, the soul too will do the same. All materialistically thinking souls work on the production of evil race-formations, and what is done of a spiritual nature causes the bringing forth of a good race. Just as humanity has brought forth creations that have retrogressed as animals, plants and minerals, so will a portion split off and represent the evil part of humanity. In the body which will meanwhile have grown soft the inner badness of the soul will express itself externally. Just as older conditions that have degenerated to the ape species seem grotesque to us today, so will materialistic races remain at the standpoint of evil, peopling the earth as evil races. It will lie entirely with the human being as to whether a soul wants to remain in the bad race or wants to ascend by spiritual culture to a good race.

These are things that we must know if we want to live into the future with real knowledge. Otherwise we go through the world blindfolded, for forces are working in humanity which we must recognize and to which we must pay attention. A person would neglect his duty to humanity if he did not wish to become acquainted with the forces that work in the direction of right evolution or against it. Knowledge for the sake of knowledge would be egoism. Those who want to know in order to look into higher worlds act egoistically. But those who try to carry this knowledge into the direct practice of everyday life, further the advance of the coming evolution of humanity. It is extremely important for us to learn more and more to put into practice what exists as the conception of spiritual science.

So you see, the spiritual movement has a quite specific goal, namely to create a mould for future humanity in advance. The goal can be reached in no other way than through the acceptance of spiritual wisdom. This is the thought that lives in the mind of one who conceives spiritual science as the great task of humanity. He thinks of it as inseparable from evolution and he regards it not as an object of desire but as a task and duty that is laid upon him. The more we acknowledge this, the more rapidly do we approach the future form of humanity in the sixth age. Just as long ago in ancient Atlantis, in the neighbourhood of modern Ireland, the advanced human beings journeyed eastwards in order to found the new civilizations, so do we now have the task of working towards the great moment in the sixth age when humanity will undertake a great spiritual ascent.

We must endeavour to come out of materialism again, and societies with a spiritual aim must undertake to guide humanity not from motives of arrogance and pride, but as a task and duty. So a certain group of people must join together in order to prepare the future. But this union is not to be conceived of geographically. All ideas of locality have lost their meaning in this connection because it is no longer a question of racial relationships. The point will be for people over the whole earth to find each other spiritually, in order to fashion the future in a positive way. For this reason, 400 years ago when our epoch plunged its deepest into matter, the Rosicrucian Brotherhood laid emphasis on that practical spiritual science which contains an answer to all problems of everyday life.

Here you have the ascending evolution to counterbalance the descending one. Just as old knowledge acts as a dividing force, as is shown by Mauthner's *Critique of Language*, so the spiritual current of thought seeks the unifying bond of spiritual wisdom. Hence arises the new schooling of initiation which is directly concerned with leading humanity over into a new cycle of time.

In this way the concept of initiation is connected with the principle of human evolution.

# Lecture 14

# The Nature of Initiation

Today we shall speak about the principle of initiation, or esoteric training. We will speak of the two schooling methods which take into special consideration what has been explained here concerning human evolution, for we must be clear that in a certain way we find the truth by retracing our steps to earlier stages of humanity.

We said that the inhabitants of old Atlantis could perceive wisdom in all that surrounded them. The further back we go into the far past, the more do we find states of consciousness through which human beings were able to perceive the creative powers that pervade the world, and the spiritual beings who surround us. All that surrounds us has arisen through these creative beings, and to see them is indeed the meaning of knowing.

When humanity had developed to our present stage of consciousness (and this has only come about during our fifth post-Atlantean epoch) a longing was left in the soul to penetrate again into spiritual realms. I have told you how in the ancient Indian people there lived from the beginning a deep longing to know the real spirit behind all that surrounds us in the world. We have seen how they had a feeling that all that surrounded them was a dream, an illusion; how their only task was to evolve upwards to the ancient wisdom that had worked creatively in early times. The pupils of the ancient Rishis strove to tread the path that led them through yoga to look up into the realms from which they had themselves come down. They strove to escape from *maya* to these spiritual realms above.

That is one path which we can take. But the newest way of attaining wisdom is the Rosicrucian path. This path does not point us to the past but to the future, to those conditions that we will still live through. Through precise methods the pupil is taught to develop in himself the wisdom that exists as a seed in every human being. This is the way that was given through the founder of the Rosicrucian esoteric stream, known to the outer world as Christian Rosenkreuz. It is not an un-Christian way, but rather a Christian path adapted to modern conditions, and it lies between the actual Christian path and the yoga path. This path had been partially prepared long before the time of Christianity. It took on a special form through the great initiate, Dionysius the Areopagite, who in the esoteric school of Paul at Athens inaugurated the training from which all later esoteric wisdom and training have been derived.

These are the two paths of esoteric training particularly fitted for the West. All that is connected with our culture and the life we lead and must lead, is lifted up, raised into the principle of initiation through the Christian and through the Rosicrucian training. The purely Christian way is somewhat difficult for modern human beings, hence the Rosicrucian path has been introduced for those who have to live in the present age. If someone wants to take the old, purely Christian path in the midst of modern life, he must be able to cut himself off for a time from the world outside, in order to enter it again later all the more intensely. On the other hand the Rosicrucian path can be followed by all, no matter in what occupation or sphere of life they may be placed.

Let us describe the purely Christian way. Its method is prescribed in the most profound Christian book—least understood by the representatives of Christian theology—the Gospel of John. Its content is also to be found in the Apocalypse or Secret Revelation.

The Gospel of John is a miraculous book: one must live it, not merely read it. One can live it if one understands that its utterances are precepts for the inner life, and that one must observe them in the right way. The Christian path demands of its disciple that he consider the Gospel of John a book of meditation. A fundamental assumption, which is more or less absent in Rosicrucian teaching, is that one possesses the most steadfast belief in the personality of Christ Jesus. The pupil must at least believe in the possibility that the most lofty Being, the Leader of the Fire-Spirits of Sun evolution, was physically incarnated as Jesus of Nazareth; that Christ Jesus was not merely the 'ordinary man of Nazareth', not an individual like Socrates, Plato or Pythagoras. One must see his fundamental difference from all others. If one wants to undergo a purely Christian training one must be sure that in him lived a God-man of unique stature, otherwise one has not the right basic feeling that enters the soul and awakens it. Therefore one must have a genuine belief in the first words of the Gospel of John: 'In the beginning was the Logos and the Logos was with God and a God was the Logos,' and on to the words, 'And the Logos became flesh and dwelt among us.' Thus the same Spirit who was the ruler of the Fire-Spirits, who was linked with the transforming of Earth, whom we also call the Spirit of the Earth, has actually dwelt among us in a garment of flesh; he was actually in a physical body. That must be recognized. If one cannot do this then it is better to undertake another method of schooling. Someone, however, who has accepted this basic condition and every morning, through weeks and months, calls before his soul in meditation the Gospel words down to the passage 'full of grace and truth', and moreover in such a way that he not only understands them, but lives within them, will experience them as an awakening force in his soul. For these are not ordinary words, but awakening forces which call forth other forces in the soul.

The pupil must only have the patience to bring them before his soul continuously, every day, and they will become the forces that Christian schooling needs, aroused through the awakening of quite definite feelings. The Christian path is a more inward one, whereas in Rosicrucian training experiences are kindled by the outer world.

The Christian path is accomplished through an awakening of the feelings. There are seven stages of feeling that must be aroused. In addition there are other exercises that are only given personally to the pupil, and suited to his or her special character. It is, however, indispensable to experience the thirteenth chapter of the John Gospel in the manner I will now describe. The teacher says to the pupil: You must develop certain specific feelings. Imagine the following: the plant grows from the soil, but it is of a higher order than the mineral soil from which it grows. Nevertheless the plant needs it; the higher could not exist without the lower, and if the plant could think, it would have to say to the earth: It is true that I am higher than you, yet without you I cannot live. It ought to bow down to the earth in gratitude. Likewise must the animal bear itself towards the plant, for it could not exist without plant life. And even so must the human being bear himself with regard to the animal. If a human being has ascended higher, he must say to himself: I could never stand where I do without the lower. He must bow down in gratitude before it, for it has made it possible for him to exist. No creature in the world could exist without the lower, to which it must feel gratitude. Even Christ, the very highest, could not exist without the twelve, and the feeling of his bowing before them in gratitude is powerfully portrayed in this thirteenth chapter. He, the highest of all, washes his disciples' feet.

If you imagine this basic feeling awakening in the human soul, if the pupil lives for weeks and months in reflection and contemplation that deepen this fundamental feeling—the gratitude with which the higher should look down to the lower to which it really owes its existence—then one awakens the first basic feeling. The pupil will have entered deeply enough into the experience when certain symptoms appear, an external symptom and an inner vision. The external symptom is that one feels one's feet to be laved by water; in an inner vision one sees oneself as the Christ washing the feet of the twelve. This is the first stage, that of the Washing of the Feet. The event in the thirteenth chapter of the John Gospel is not only an historical event; it can be experienced by anyone. It is an external symptomatic expression of the fact that the pupil has raised himself thus far in his life of feeling, nor does this sign fail to appear when he has progressed to this point in the enhancement of his feeling-life.

The second stage, the Scourging, is passed through if one immerses oneself in the following: How would it fare with me if the sufferings and blows of life broke in on me from every side? I must stand upright, I must make myself strong to meet all the sorrows that life offers, and must bear them. This is the second fundamental feeling that must be experienced. The outer feeling of it is an irritation on the whole surface of the body, and a more inner expression is a vision in which one sees oneself scourged, at first in dream, and then in vision.

Then comes the third, which is the Crowning with Thorns. Here, week-long, month-long one must live in the feeling: How would it fare with me if I must not only undergo the sorrows and sufferings of life, but even if the holiest, my spiritual being, should be subjected to scorn and derision? Again, there must be no lamenting, it must be clear to the pupil that he must stand upright in spite of everything. His inwardly developed strength must make him able to stand erect despite mockery and scorn. Whatever threatens to overthrow his soul, he must stand firm. Then in an inner astral vision he sees himself with the crown of thorns and is sensible of an external pain on the head. This is the sign that he has advanced far enough in his life of feeling to be able to have these experiences.

The fourth is the Crucifixion. Here the pupil must again develop a specific feeling. Today people identify their body with their ego. Someone who wants to go through Christian initiation must accustom himself to carry his body through the world as if it were a foreign object, a table, for example. His body must become foreign to him; he carries it in through the doorway and out again like something external to himself. When a pupil has advanced far enough in this fundamental feeling, there is revealed to him what is called the Ordeal of the Blood. Certain reddenings of the skin appear on certain places in such a way that he can call forth the wounds of Christ on hands and feet and on the right side of the chest. When the pupil by his warmth of feeling is able to develop in himself the Ordeal of the Blood, the external symptoms, then in his inner being, the astral, he sees himself crucified.

The fifth is the Mystic Death. The pupil raises himself ever higher to the feeling: I belong to the whole world; I am as little an independent being as the finger on my hand. He feels himself embedded in the whole world, as if a part of it. Then he experiences the feeling that all around him grows dark, as if a black darkness were enveloping him, like a pall that becomes dense around him. During this time the pupil of Christian initiation comes to know all the sorrow and all the pain, all the evil and wickedness that attaches itself to mortal creatures. That is the Descent into Hell; each one must live through it. Then something comes to pass as if the veil were torn asunder, and the pupil sees into the spiritual worlds. This is called the Rending of the Veil.

The sixth is the Burial and Resurrection. When the pupil has advanced thus far he must say: I have already accustomed myself to look on my body as something foreign, but now I see everything in the world as close to me as my own body, which indeed is only taken from these substances. Every flower, every stone, is as near to me as my body. Then the pupil is buried in the earthly planet. This stage is necessarily linked with a new life, with the feeling of being united with the deepest soul of the planet, with the soul of the Christ, who says, 'Those who eat my bread tread me underfoot.'

The seventh, the Ascension, cannot be described; one must have a soul that is no longer dependent on thinking through the instrument of the brain. In order to be sensible of what the pupil undergoes in what is called the Ascension, it is necessary to have a soul that can live through this feeling.

This passing through states of humility and deep devotion represents the nature of the Christian initiation, and someone who earnestly goes through it experiences his resurrection in the spiritual worlds. Today it is not possible for all to undertake this path, and so the existence of another method leading to higher worlds has become a necessity. That is the Rosicrucian method.

Here again I must refer to seven stages that will give a picture of the content of this training. Much of it has already been described in the periodical *Luzifer-Gnosis*, much can only be given from teacher to pupil within the schooling process, and yet an idea must be formed of what the training provides.[38] It has seven stages, though not consecutive; it is a question of the pupil's own individuality. The teacher prescribes what seems to him adapted to his pupil, and much else forms a part that cannot be made public.

The seven stages are as follows:

1. Study.
2. Imaginative Knowledge.
3. Inspired Knowledge, or Reading the Esoteric Script.
4. Preparing the Philosopher's Stone.

5. Correspondence between Macrocosm and Microcosm.
6. Living into the Macrocosm.
7. Divine Bliss.

Study in the Rosicrucian sense is the ability to immerse oneself in the content of thought not taken from physical reality but from higher worlds. This is called the life in pure thought. Modern philosophers for the most part deny this; they say that every kind of thinking must have some vestige remaining from sense perception. This, however, is not the case, for no one, for example, can see a true circle; a circle must be seen in the mind; on the blackboard it is only a collection of tiny particles of chalk. One can only attain to a real circle if one leaves aside all examples, all actual things. Thus thinking in mathematics is a supersensible activity. But one must also learn to think supersensibly in other fields.

Initiates have always exercised this kind of thinking in regard to the human being. Rosicrucian wisdom is such a supersensible knowledge, and its study, with which we are now occupied, is the first stage of the Rosicrucian training itself. I am not describing Rosicrucian wisdom for any external reason, but because it is the first stage of Rosicrucian initiation.

People often enough think it unnecessary to talk about the members of the human being, or the evolution of humanity or the different planetary evolutions; they would prefer to acquire beautiful feelings rather than study seriously. Nevertheless, however many beautiful feelings one acquires in one's soul, it is impossible to rise into the spiritual worlds by that means alone. Rosicrucian wisdom does not try to arouse the feelings, but through the stupendous facts of the spiritual worlds to let the feelings themselves begin to resound. The Rosicrucian feels it a kind of impertinence to take people by storm with feelings. He leads them along the path of humanity's evolution in the belief that feelings will then arise of themselves. He calls up before them the planet journeying in universal space, knowing that when the soul experiences this fact it will be powerfully gripped in feeling. It is only an empty phrase to say one should address oneself directly to the feelings; that is just indolence. Rosicrucian wisdom lets the facts speak, and if these thoughts flow into the feeling nature and overpower it, then that is the right way. Only what the human being feels of his own accord can fill him with bliss or blessedness. The Rosicrucian lets the facts in the cosmos speak, for that is the most impersonal kind of teaching. It is a matter of indifference who stands before you; you must not be affected by a personality, but by what he tells you of the facts of world-evolution. Thus direct veneration of the teacher is eliminated in Rosicrucian training. The teacher neither claims it nor requires it. He wishes to speak to the pupil of what exists, quite apart from himself.

Someone who wants to press forward into the higher worlds must accustom himself to the kind of thinking in which one thought proceeds from another. A thinking of this nature is developed in my books *The Philosophy of Spiritual Activity* and *Truth and Knowledge*.[39] These books are not written in a way that enables one to extract a thought and place it elsewhere; they are written as an organism arises, one thought grows out of another. These books have nothing at all to do with the person who wrote them; he gave himself up to what the thoughts themselves worked out in him, how they linked themselves to one another.

Thus for someone desiring to make a beginning, study means acquiring a degree of knowledge of the elementary facts of spiritual science itself, whereas for someone who wishes to go further it means inner meditation in a thought-structure which lets one thought grow out of another, out of itself.

The second stage is Imaginative Knowledge, the knowledge which unites with what is given to the pupil at the study stage. Study is the basis, which must be perfected through individual imaginative knowledge. If you think over various things I touched on in the previous lectures, you will find traces of what were everyday occurrences on Saturn. It is possible to look on all that is around us as the physiognomy of an inner spiritual element. People walk about on the earth and it is a conglomeration of rocks and stones to them, but they must learn to grasp that everything surrounding them is a true physical expression of the Spirit of the Earth. Just as the body is ensouled, so is the earth planet the external expression for an indwelling spirit. Only when people view the earth as possessing body and soul, as the human being does, do they have an idea of what Goethe meant when he said: 'All things corruptible are but a semblance.'[40] When you see tears run down a human face you do not apply the laws of physics to examine how quickly or slowly the tears roll down; they express the inner sadness of the soul, just as a smile is the expression of the soul's inner joy. The pupil must educate himself to see in every single flower in a meadow the outer expression of a living being, the expression of the Spirit dwelling in the earth. Some flowers seem to be tears, others are the joyful expression of the earth's Spirit. Every stone, every plant, every flower is for the pupil the outer expression of the indwelling Earth Spirit, its physiognomy that speaks to him. Everything 'corruptible' or transitory becomes a 'semblance' of something eternal, expressing itself through it.

Feelings like these had to be attained by the disciple of the Grail, and by the Rosicrucian. The teacher would say: See the flower chalice which receives the ray of sunlight; the sun calls forth the pure productive forces that slumber in the plant and hence the sun's ray was called the 'holy lance of love'. Now see the human being; he is more exalted than the plant, he has the same organs within him, but all that the plant harbours in itself, perfectly pure and chaste, is in him steeped in lust and impure desire. The future of human evolution consists in this: the human being will again be chaste and pure, and speak forth his likeness into the world through another organ which will be the transformed organ of generation. The human generative organ will be chaste and pure without desire, without passion; and as the calyx of the blossom turns upward to the holy love lance, it will turn to the spiritual ray of wisdom, and fructified by this will bring forth its own image. This organ will be the larynx.

The Grail pupil was shown: The plant at its lower stage has this pure chalice, the human being has lost it; he has degenerated to impure desires. Out of the spiritualized sun-ray he must let this chalice arise again; in chastity he must develop that which forms the Holy Grail of the future.

Thus the pupil looks up to the great ideal. What comes to pass in the slow evolution of the whole human race is experienced in advance by the initiate. He shows us humanity's evolution in pictures and these pictures work quite differently from the abstract thoughts that have been produced by the modern materialistic age. If you imagine evolution in such lofty and powerful pictures as the Grail, then the effect is different from that of ordinary knowledge, which is unable to exercise any deep influence on your organism. Imaginative knowledge works down to the ether body and thence on to the blood, and this is the medium which acts formatively on the organism. The human being will become increasingly more able to work on his organism through his ether body. All imaginative knowledge based on truth is at the same time healing and health-giving; it makes the blood healthy in its circulation. The best teacher is imaginative knowledge, if only the human being is strong and devoted enough for it to be able to work on him.

The third stage is Reading the Esoteric Script, that is, not only seeing isolated pictures but letting the interrelationship of these pictures work upon one. This becomes what is called the esoteric script. One begins to co-ordinate the lines of force which stream creatively through the world, forming them into definite figures and colour-forms through Imagination. One learns to discover an inner connection that is expressed in these figures, and this acts as spiritual sound, as the harmony of the spheres, for the figures are founded on true cosmic proportions. Our writing is a last decadent relic of this old esoteric script and is modelled on it.

We come to the fourth stage, Preparing the Philosopher's Stone, through exercises of the breathing process. When we breathe in a natural way we need the plant-world for our breathing. If plants were not there we could not live, for they give us oxygen and assimilate the carbon we breathe out. The plant builds up its own organism from this and gives back oxygen; thus oxygen is continually renewed for us by the plant world. Humanity could not exist by itself; eliminate the plant world and humanity would die out in a short time. You see the cycle: you inhale oxygen which the plant exhales, you exhale carbon which the plant inhales and from which it builds up its own bodily nature. Thus the plant belongs to us; it is the instrument by which our life is sustained. You may see in coal how the plant builds its body from carbon, for coal is nothing other than the dead remains of plants.

Rosicrucian training guides the pupil through a specifically regulated breathing process to form the organ that can effect the transformation of carbon into oxygen within him. What is today done by the plant externally will, later on, through a future organ which the pupil is already developing by means of his training, be effected in the human being himself. This is slowly being prepared. Through the regulated breathing process the human being will bear in himself the instrument for preparing oxygen; he will have become akin to the plant, whereas now he is of a mineral nature. He will retain the carbon in himself and build his body from it, and hence his body will later on be more plant-like; then he can turn to meet the holy lance of love. The whole of humanity will then possess a consciousness like that gained by the initiate today, when he raises himself into higher worlds.

This is called the transmutation of human substance into that substance of which carbon itself is the basis. This is the alchemy that leads the human being to build up his own body as does the plant today. One calls this the Preparation of the Philosopher's Stone, and carbon is the outer symbol. But it is not the Philosopher's Stone until the pupil can create it himself through his regulated breathing process. The teaching can only be given from teacher to pupil; it is wrapped in deep secrecy, and only after he is completely purified and made ready can the pupil receive this mystery. If it were to be made public today, then human beings in their egoism would gratify their lowest needs through the misuse of this highest mystery.

The fifth stage is the Correspondence of Macrocosm and Microcosm. When we survey the path of human evolution we see that what lies within the human being today has gradually entered from without—for instance, the glands were an external growth on Sun, like our modern fungi; all that today lies within the human skin was once outside. The human body is, in a way, pieced together from what was spread outside it. Each separate member of your physical body, ether body and astral body was somewhere outside in the universe. This is the macrocosm in the microcosm. Your very soul was outside in the Godhead. Whatever is within us corresponds to something that is outside, and we must learn to know these true correspondences in ourselves.

You are familiar with the spot on the brow just above the root of the nose. It expresses the fact that a certain something which was formerly outside has withdrawn inside. If you penetrate this organ in meditation, sink yourself into it, this denotes more than a mere brooding in this point; you learn to know the part of the outer world that corresponds to it. The larynx, too, you get to know, and the forces that build it. Thus you learn about the macrocosm through immersing yourself in your own body.

This is no mere brooding within yourself. You should not say: God is within and I will see him. You would only find the puny human being whom you yourself magnify into God. Someone who only speaks of this inward brooding never comes to real knowledge. To reach this by the path of Rosicrucian wisdom is less comfortable and demands real work. The universe is full of beautiful and marvellous things; one must be absorbed in these, one must seek God in his individual expressions. Then one can find him in oneself and only then does one learn to know God as One. The world is like a great book. We find its letters in created things; we must read these from beginning to end, and then we learn to read the book microcosm and the book macrocosm from beginning to end.

This is no longer mere understanding; it lives in feelings, it fuses the human being with the whole universe and he feels all things to be the expression of the divine Spirit of the Earth. If someone has reached this point, he voluntarily performs all his deeds in accordance with the will of the whole cosmos, and this is what is known as Divine Bliss.

When we are able to think in this way, we are treading the Rosicrucian path. Christian schooling is based more on the development of inner feelings. In Rosicrucian schooling all that is spread out in physical reality as the divine nature of the earth is allowed to work upon us and reverberate in us as feeling. These are two paths that are open to all. If you think in the manner of modern thought, then you can take the Rosicrucian path, no matter how scientific you may be. Modern science is an assistance if you do not merely study cosmic evolution by reading the letters, as it were, but carry your research into what is concealed behind them, just as in a book one does not consider the separate letters but reads the meaning by their aid. You must seek the spirit behind science, then science becomes for you simply the letters which convey the spirit.

What has been said is not meant to be a comprehensive account of Rosicrucian training. It is only meant to serve as an indication of what can be found in it. It is a path for the present-day human being; it makes him capable of working into the future. These are only the elementary stages, to give some idea of the path. We can thus realize how the Rosicrucian method enables us to penetrate into the higher mysteries.

Spiritual science is necessary to humanity for its further progress. What is to take place for the transformation of humanity must be brought about through human beings themselves. Someone who accepts the truth in his present incarnation will mould for himself in later incarnations the outer form for the deeper truths.

Thus what we have discussed in these lectures is an inter-related whole. It is the instrument which is to work creatively for future civilization. It is taught today because the human being of the future needs these teachings, because they must be introduced into the evolutionary path of humanity. Everyone who will not accept this truth of the future lives at the cost of others. But those who accept it live for others, even if at first they are impelled by an egoistic longing for the higher worlds. If the path is the right one then it is of itself the destroyer of self-seeking and the best teacher of selflessness.

Spiritual development is now needed by humanity and must be implanted into it. An earnest, true endeavour for truth, step by step—this alone leads to genuine brotherliness, this is the magician who can best bring about the uniting of humanity. This will serve as the means to bring about humanity's great goal, unity. We shall reach this goal if we develop the means to it in ourselves, if we seek to acquire these means in the noblest, purest way, for it is a matter of hallowing humanity through these means.

Thus spiritual science appears to us not only as a great ideal, but as a force with which we permeate ourselves and out of which knowledge wells up for us. Spiritual science will become increasingly more widespread, it will penetrate more and more all the religious and practical aspects of life, just as the great law of existence penetrates all beings; it is a factor in humanity's evolution.

This is the sense in which these lectures on Rosicrucian wisdom have been given. If this has been understood, not only abstractly, but so that feelings have been evoked through knowledge of facts, then it can work directly into life. When this knowledge involves us fully, flows from head to heart and thence to hands, into all that we do and create, then we have grasped the foundations of spiritual science. Then we have grasped the great task of civilization that is placed into our hands, and then from this knowledge feelings, too, are developed, feelings that those who like to take things easily would prefer to develop direct.

Rosicrucian wisdom does not wish to revel in feelings, it wishes to present you with the facts of the spirit. The pupil must take part, must let himself be stimulated by the facts which have been described. Feelings and sensations must be aroused in him through facts. In this sense spiritual science should become a powerful impulse for the sphere of feeling, but at the same time be something that leads us directly into the facts of supersensible perceptions, which lets them first arise as thoughts and then leads the seeker upward into the higher world.

This was the intended purpose of these lectures.

# Notes

The only record of the German text of these lectures is a combined version of notes taken by Camille Wandrey and Walther Vegelahn. Rudolf Steiner did not check these notes.

1   Gottfried Wilhelm Leibniz (1646-1716), founder of monadology and differential and integral calculus.
2   Gotthold Ephraim Lessing (1729-1781), critic, poet and thinker. *The Education of the Human Race* (1780) (London: Anthroposophical Publishing Company, 1927).
3   Johann Wolfgang von Goethe (1749-1832). On his initiation see in particular R. Steiner, *The Karma of Vocation* (GA 172). (Tr. O. D. Wannamaker, rev. G. Church. New York: Anthroposophic Press, 1984).
4   See: R. Steiner, *The Mysteries* (in GA 98). (London: Rudolf Steiner Publishing Company, 1946).
5   See: R. Steiner, *Goethe's Standard of the Soul* (GA 22). (Tr. D. Osmond. London: Anthroposophical Publishing Company, 1925). Chapters II and III.
6   Bernoulli: a family of scientists and mathematicians in Basle, Switzerland.
7   Pictured in: R. Steiner, *Occult Signs and Symbols* (in GA 284). (Tr. S. Kurland & G. Church. New York: Anthroposophic Press, 1975).
8   At this point the extant German text names 'manas, buddhi, atma'.
9   W. Scott-Elliot (W. Williamson), author of *Legends of Atlantis and Lost Lemuria* (1896 & 1904), (Wheaton USA: Theosophical Publishing House, Quest Books, 1990).
10  Adelbert von Chamisso (1781-1838): *Peter Schlemihls wundersame Geschichte* (The strange tale of Peter Schlemihl), 1814.

11   At this point the extant German text has 'rank and race hatred', probably a mishearing of German 'Klassen' (class) for 'Rassen' (race), as the latter makes no sense in this context.

12   Russo-Japanese War: 1904-1905.

13   Fabre d'Olivet (1768-1825), author of *La langue hébraique restitué* (Paris 1816), and *Histoire philosophique du genre humain* (Paris 1822).

14   Goethe *Faust, A Tragedy*, (Tr. Bayard Taylor. London: Frederick Warne & Co, no date). Part II, Act 1, A gloomy Gallery.

15   Goethe *Faust, A Tragedy*, op. cit. Part I, Scene III, The Study: 'The lord of rats and eke of mice,/Of flies and bed-bugs, frogs and lice.'

16   Johann Sebastian Bach (1685-1750).

17   R. Steiner, *The Occult Significance of Blood* (in GA 55). (London: Rudolf Steiner Press, 1967). Lecture of 25 October 1906.

18   Steiner subsequently used the term 'Imagination' for this level of consciousness.

19   This translation from *The Complete Poetical Works of Percy Bysshe Shelley*, Ed. T. Hutchinson, (London: Oxford University Press, 1956).

20   Steiner subsequently used the term 'Intuition' for this level of consciousness.

21   Spirits of Egoism: called Archai or Spirits of Personality in R. Steiner, *Occult Science: an Outline* (GA 13). (Tr. G. & M. Adams. London: Rudolf Steiner Press, 1984).

22   John, 13,18.

23   The eighth: The list of members of the human being begins with the physical body as the first. Hence the member mentioned here is counted as the eighth. See description in Lecture 9.

24   Lunar Pitri is the name given to these beings in theosophical literature, which has its roots in India (cf. H. P. Blavatsky's *The Secret Doctrine*).

25   Goethe *Faust, A Tragedy*, op. cit. Part I, Scene IV, The Study: 'A little burning air, which I shall soon prepare/Above the earth will nimbly bear us.'

26   The extant notes here say 'millions of years'.

27   Fritz Mauthner (1849-1923), *Beiträge zu einer Kritik der Sprache* (3 vols.), 1901/2.
28   Genesis 2,7.
29   The extant notes here say 'millions of years'.
30   The fossilized remains of dinosaurs date from the Triassic, Jurassic and Cretaceous periods which correspond to the Lemurian age of the earth.
31   Genesis 1, 2.
32   Laocoon group (42-21BC) by three Rhodian sculptors: now in the Belvedere Palace of the Vatican.
33   Luke 14,26 and Matthew 19, 29.
34   The extant notes here say 'millions of years'.
35   The extant notes here say 'millions of years'.
36   This is a much simplified sketch of very complicated processes.
37   Genesis 1, 26.
38   These essays were published in 1909 in R. Steiner, *Knowledge of the Higher Worlds* (GA 10). (Tr. D. Osmond & C. Davy. London: Rudolf Steiner Press, 1985). Also available as: *How to Know Higher Worlds* (Tr. C. Bamford. New York: Anthroposophic Press, 1994). The same schooling path is also described in the chapter 'Knowledge of Higher Worlds' in *Occult Science: an Outline* (GA 13). (Tr. G. & M. Adams. London: Rudolf Steiner Press, 1984).
39   R. Steiner, *The Philosophy of Spiritual Activity: A Philosophy of Freedom* (GA 4). (Tr. rev. R. Stebbing. Forest Row, Sussex: Rudolf Steiner Press, 1992). R. Steiner, *Truth and Knowledge. An Introduction to Philosophy of Spiritual Activity* (GA 3). (Tr. R. Stebbing. New York: Steinerbooks, 1981).
40   Goethe, *Faust, A Tragedy*, op. cit. Part II, Act V, Chorus Mysticus.

# Publisher's Note Regarding
# Rudolf Steiner's Lectures

The lectures and addresses contained in this volume have been translated from the German, which is based on stenographic and other recorded texts that were in most cases never seen or revised by the lecturer. Hence, due to human errors in hearing and transcription, they may contain mistakes and faulty passages. Every effort has been made to ensure that this is not the case. Some of the lectures were given to audiences more familiar with anthroposophy; these are the so-called 'private' or 'members' lectures. Other lectures, like the written works, were intended for the general public. The difference between these, as Rudolf Steiner indicates in his *Autobiography*, is twofold. On the one hand, the lectures given to members of the Anthroposophical Society take for granted a background in and commitment to anthroposophy; in the public lectures this was not the case. At the same time, the members' lectures address the concerns and dilemmas of the members, while the public work speaks directly out of Steiner's own understanding of universal needs. Nevertheless, as Rudolf Steiner stresses: 'Nothing was ever said that was not solely the result of my direct experience of the growing content of anthroposophy. There was never any question of concessions to the prejudices and preferences of the members. Whoever reads these privately printed lectures can take them to represent anthroposophy in the fullest sense. Thus it was possible without hesitation—when the complaints in this direction became too persistent—to depart from the custom of circulating this material "for members only". But it must be borne in mind that faulty passages do occur in these reports not revised by myself.' Earlier in the same chapter, he states: 'Had I been able to correct them [the private lectures], the restriction *for members only* would have been unnecessary from the beginning.'